Explorations in Language Acquisition and Use

Explorations in Language Acquisition and Use

THE TAIPEI LECTURES

Stephen D. Krashen

HEINEMANN
Portsmouth, NH

Heinemann

361 Hanover Street
Portsmouth, NH 03801–3912
www.heinemann.com

Offices and agents throughout the world

Library of Congress Cataloging-in-Publication Data
Krashen, Stephen D.
    Explorations in language acquisition and use : the Taipei lectures / Stephen Krashen.
      p.   cm.
    Includes bibliographical references and index.
      ISBN 0-325-00554-0
    1. Language and languages—Study and teaching.   2. Language acquisition.   I. Title.

P51 .K666   2003
418′.0071—dc21   2002013703

Editor: Lois Bridges
Production: Elizabeth Valway
Cover design: Joni Doherty
Typesetter: TechBooks
Manufacturing: Steve Bernier

Printed in the United States of America on acid-free paper
Sheridan 2018

Contents

INTRODUCTION   *vii*

1   **Principles of Language Acquisition**   *1*
    Part 1: Theory   *1*
    Part 2: Applications   *6*
    Notes   *14*

2   **Free Voluntary Reading: Still a Very Good Idea**   *15*
    Research on Free Reading   *15*
    Light Reading As a Bridge   *22*
    Other Advantages of Reading   *22*
    Motivating Students to Read   *24*
    Some Innovations   *25*
    Conclusion   *26*
    Notes   *26*

3   **Current Issues and Controversies: Does Grammar Teaching
    Work? What About "Comprehensible Output"?**   *30*
    The Role of Grammar   *30*
    Comprehensible Output?   *59*
    Notes   *65*

4   **How Reading and Writing Make You Smarter, or, How Smart
    People Read and Write**   *68*
    How We Get Smart   *68*
    Some Notes on Incubation   *69*
    The Research on Learning by Problem Solving   *70*
    Reading and Cognitive Development   *72*
    Writing and Cognitive Development   *73*
    Oral Language   *77*
    Conclusion   *78*
    Obstacles   *79*
    Notes   *80*

CONCLUSION   *83*

REFERENCES   *87*

INDEX   *97*

Introduction

On November 17 and 18, 2001, I presented a series of four lectures at National Taipei University in Taiwan. I attempted to review the fundamentals of second-language acquisition theory, present some of the original research supporting the theory as well as more recent studies, present counterarguments to criticisms, and explore some new areas that appear to have promise for progress in both theory and application. This volume is based on these lectures. Chapters 1, 2, and 4 correspond closely to three of the four lectures presented. Chapter 3 includes material presented in the fourth lecture but also includes material discussed in response to questions from the audience, as well as a discussion of a recent paper by Norris and Ortega dealing with the effect of grammar instruction.

Chapter 1 reviews the central hypotheses underlying what I consider to be current theory in language acquisition. These hypotheses have not only survived well over the years but have also proven to be useful in other areas of language education. So far, research results remain consistent with these hypotheses and there is no counterevidence. According to the rules of science, this is all one can demand of a hypothesis. But the fact that the hypotheses have also helped explain phenomena in other areas is equally impressive. The clearest example is the role of the input hypothesis (also known as the comprehension hypothesis). As explored in Chapter 2, the input hypothesis has been successfully applied in the area of reading; comprehensible input in the form of free voluntary reading has been shown to be highly effective for first- and second-language development. I have argued in other publications that comprehensible input also helps explain the success of whole language methodology in beginning reading (Krashen 1999a) as well as the success of well-designed bilingual education programs (Krashen 1996).

Chapter 3 is self-defense. The research community has devoted an extraordinary amount of energy in an attempt to show that grammar teaching works. Instead, they have shown only what many, many language students have always realized: Formal grammar instruction has a very limited impact on second-language competence. Even intensive, prolonged instruction that is limited to just a few aspects of grammar results, in general, in only modest gains on tests in which students are encouraged to think about form. The researchers themselves, in every case, consider their results to strongly support the efficacy of grammar instruction. I argue in Chapter 3 that the results only show that the Monitor hypothesis, reviewed in Chapter 1, is correct.

Chapter 3 also contains a discussion of a current rival to the input hypothesis, the comprehensible output hypothesis. Its originator, Merrill Swain, did not consider it to be a rival, but rather a supplement to comprehensible input. Yet much of current practice assumes the correctness of comprehensible output and considers it to be the major path to second-language competence. The data, in my view, certainly does not support comprehensible output as the only way; in fact, there is little evidence that it plays any role at all. Parts of Chapter 3 were originally published in *Foreign Language Annals* (Krashen 1999b) and *System* (Krashen 1998).

Chapter 4 is an exploration into other areas. Good readers and writers, I argue, are those who have learned to read and write in a way that is consistent with the way the brain learns and solves problems. Unfortunately, the most efficient ways of using reading and writing are often different from the way we are taught in school. Good thinkers, I conclude, are those who have overcome the lessons they have learned in school. A previous version of this paper was originally presented at the Georgetown Round Table on Languages and Linguistics and was published in their proceedings (Krashen 1990). It has been updated and, I hope, improved by the addition of recent work on the composing process, especially the interesting work of Robert Boice. Boice's insights have, in fact, been of great help to me in completing this manuscript. I highly recommend his 1994 book, *How Writers Journey to Comfort and Fluency*.

I thank my former student and now valued colleague Professor Sy-ying Lee of National Taipei University, who organized the series of presentations in Taiwan. I also thank the chair of the department of Foreign Languages and Applied Linguistics at National Taipei University, Professor Ching-kang Liu, for his hospitality.

1

Principles of Language Acquisition

Part 1: Theory

The following five hypotheses are the core of current theory on language acquisition. They are presented here as a summary without supporting evidence. For much more detail, see Krashen (1981, 1982, 1985, 1994a), Krashen and Terrell (1983).

The Acquisition-Learning Hypothesis

The acquisition-learning hypothesis claims that we have two independent ways of developing language ability: acquisition and learning.

Language *acquisition* is a subconscious process; while it is happening, we are not aware that it is happening. Also, once we have acquired something, we are not usually aware that we possess any new knowledge; the knowledge is stored in our brains subconsciously. The research strongly supports the view that both children and adults can subconsciously acquire language. Also, both oral and written language can be acquired. In nontechnical language, acquisition is sometimes referred to as "picking up" a language. When someone says, "I was in France for a while and I picked up some French," it means he or she acquired some French.

Language *learning* is what we did in school. It is a conscious process; when we are learning, we know we are learning. Also, learned knowledge is represented consciously in the brain. In nontechnical language, when we talk about "rules" and "grammar," we are usually talking about learning.

Error correction helps learning. When we make a mistake and someone corrects us, we are supposed to change our conscious version of the rule. If a learner says, "I comes to school every day," and a teacher responds with, "No, it's 'I *come* to school,' " the learner is supposed to realize that the -s doesn't go on the first person singular. As we shall see, error correction and conscious learning are very limited.

The Natural Order Hypothesis

The natural order hypothesis claims that we acquire the parts of a language in a predictable order. Some grammatical items, for example, tend to be acquired early, while others come later.

The order of acquisition for first and second languages is similar, but not identical. It has been established, for example, that the -*ing* marker in English, the progressive, is acquired fairly early in first-language acquisition, while the third person singular -*s* is acquired later. The third person singular may arrive six months to a year after -*ing*. In adult second-language acquisition, the progressive is also acquired early, but the third person singular may never come. It is common to hear people who speak English as a second language very well, and yet have not acquired the third person singular. Not every acquirer proceeds in exactly the same order, but the variation among acquirers is not extreme. There clearly is an "average" order of acquisition.

There are three amazing facts about the natural order phenomenon, and I will list them in their order of amazingness:

1. The natural order is not based on any obvious features of simplicity and complexity. Some rules that look simple (e.g., the third person singular) are acquired late. Others that appear to linguists to be complex are acquired early. This presents a problem to curriculum designers who present rules to language students from "simple" to "complex." A rule may seem to be simple to a linguist, but may be late-acquired.

2. The natural order cannot be changed. It is immune to deliberate teaching. We cannot alter the natural order by explanations, drills, and exercises. A teacher can drill the third person singular for weeks, but it will not be acquired until the acquirer is ready for it. This explains a great deal of the frustration language students have.

3. One might suppose that the solution to our problems is simply to teach along the natural order: we need only find out which items are naturally acquired early and teach those first, etc. The third amazing fact is that this is not the solution: The natural order is not the teaching order. I will explain why later.

The Monitor Hypothesis

The Monitor hypothesis attempts to explain how acquisition and learning are used. Language is normally produced using our acquired linguistic competence. Conscious learning has only one function: As a "Monitor" or editor.

Here is how it works: We are about to say something in another language. The form of our sentence pops into our mind, thanks to our subconsciously acquired competence. Then, just before we actually produce the sentence, just before we say it, we scan it internally, inspect it, and use our consciously learned system to correct errors.

We can also use our conscious Monitor to correct sentences after we have produced them; this is called "self-correction." (Of course, we also self-correct, or edit, using our acquired system, or our "feel" for correctness. The Monitor hypothesis claims that conscious learning has *only* this function; it does not contribute to our fluency.) While the Monitor can make a small contribution to accuracy, the research indicates that acquisition makes the major contribution. Thus, acquisition is responsible for both fluency and most of our accuracy.

It is difficult to use the Monitor. In order to use the Monitor successfully, three conditions are necessary:

1. The acquirer must know the rule. This is a very difficult condition to meet. Research linguists freely admit that they do not know all the rules of any language. Those who write grammar texts know fewer rules than the linguists. Language teachers do not teach all the rules in the texts. Even the best students don't learn all the rules that are taught, even the best students don't remember all the rules they have learned, and even the best students can't always use the rules they do remember: Many rules are too complex to apply while engaging in conversation.

2. The acquirer must be thinking about correctness, or focused on form. This is hard to do. It is hard to think about both form and meaning at the same time.

3. The acquirer must have time. For most people, normal conversation doesn't provide enough time for the use of the Monitor. A few language experts can Monitor while conversing, but these are very advanced acquirers who only need to Monitor an occasional rule here and there, and who have a special interest in the structure of language.

Research shows that Monitor use is only obvious when all three conditions are fully met. For most people, this occurs only when we give them a grammar test!

The Monitor is weak, but it is not useless. Some conscious knowledge of language can be helpful. Acquisition does not, typically, provide us with 100 percent of a language; there is often a small residue of grammar, punctuation, and spelling rules that even native speakers do not acquire, even after extensive aural and written comprehensible input. In English, these can include the *lie/lay* distinction, the *its/it's* distinction, and spelling demons such as *separate* and *commitment* (how many *t*'s?). Because our standard for written communication is 100 percent, these aspects of language need to be learned, but they make up a small part of our language competence.

We pay a price for the modest amount of accuracy we get from Monitoring. Some research shows that when we focus on form when speaking, we produce less information, and we slow down (Hulstijn and Huilstijn 1984). This can seriously disrupt conversation. Some people "over-Monitor" and are so concerned with grammar and accuracy that speech is slow and painful to produce as well as to listen to:

> The major, who had been the great fencer, did not believe in bravery, and spent much time while we sat in the machines correcting my grammar. He had complimented me on how I spoke Italian, and we talked together very easily. One day I had said that Italian seemed like such an easy language to me that I could not take a great interest in it; everything was so easy to say. "Ah yes," the major said, "Why then, do you not take up the use of grammar?" So we took up the use of grammar, and soon Italian was such a difficult language that I was afraid to talk to him until I had the grammar straight in my mind.

> *(E. Hemingway, Men Without Women, 1997 [1927], 46–47)*

The best advice is, I think, to use the conscious Monitor when it does not interfere with communication, when we have time, as in the editing phase of writing.

The Input (Comprehension) Hypothesis

The input hypothesis attempts to answer the most important question in the fields of language acquisition and language education: How does language acquisition occur? The evidence strongly supports a simple hypothesis. We acquire language in only one way: when we understand messages; that is, when we obtain "comprehensible input." We acquire language, in other words, when we understand what we hear or what we read, when we understand the message.

In recent years, I have used the term *comprehension hypothesis* to refer to the input hypothesis. *Comprehension* is a better description—mere input is not enough; it must be understood. This term also allows me to honor the lineage of the input/comprehension hypothesis: The idea is certainly not new with me. In the field of second-language acquisition, James Asher, Harris Winitz, and Robins Burling proposed similar ideas years before I did, and in the field of literacy, Frank Smith and Kenneth Goodman had proposed that we learn to read by reading, by understanding the message on the page.

Comprehensible input has been our last resort in language teaching: we have tried everything else—grammar rules, repetition drills, computers, and so on. The input hypothesis claims, however, that comprehending messages is the only way language is acquired. There is no individual variation in the fundamental process of language acquisition.

The input/comprehension hypothesis can be restated in terms of the natural order hypothesis. Let us assume a very simple version of the natural order hypothesis—that we acquire the rules of a language in a linear order: 1, 2, 3... The question of how we acquire language can be restated as: How do we move from rule 3 to rule 4, from rule 987 to rule 988? More generally, if i represents the last rule we have acquired, how do we move from i to $i + 1$, where $i + 1$ is the next structure we are ready to acquire?

The input hypothesis claims that we move from i to $i + 1$ by understanding input containing $i + 1$. We are able to do this with the help of our previously acquired linguistic competence, as well as our extra-linguistic knowledge, which includes our knowledge of the world and our knowledge of the situation. In other words, we use context. (For a more detailed discussion of the role of context, including the issue of what happens when context is "too rich," and no linguistic processing is necessary, see Krashen 1999a.) For beginners, pictures are a tremendous help in making input comprehensible, as are the body movements that are at the core of Asher's Total Physical Response (TPR) method.

Now that we have some of idea of the input/comprehension hypothesis, I can share two mystical, amazing facts about language acquisition. First, language acquisition is effortless. It involves no energy, no work. All an acquirer has to do is understand messages. Second, language acquisition is involuntary. Given comprehensible input and a lack of affective barriers (see below), language acquisition will take place. The acquirer has no choice. In a theoretical sense, language teaching is easy: All we have to do is give students comprehensible messages that they will pay attention to, and they will pay attention if the messages are interesting.

Corollaries of the Input/Comprehension Hypothesis

If the input hypothesis is correct, the following corollaries are correct:

Talking is not practicing

The input hypothesis maintains that speaking does not directly result in language acquisition: talking is not practicing. If you practice your French out loud every morning in front of the mirror, your French will not improve. Rather, the ability to speak is the *result* of language acquisition, not a cause. Speaking can help language acquisition indirectly, however. First, it can result in conversation, and conversation is an excellent source of comprehensible input, even though what counts in conversation, however, is what the other person says to you, not what you say to them. I suspect that speaking can help in another way: It can make you feel more like a user of the second language, like a member of the "club." I return to this argument a bit later, in the section on the affective filter.

Given enough comprehensible input, i+1 is present

The second corollary states that if we provide students with enough comprehensible input, the structures they are ready to acquire will be present in the input. We don't have to make sure they are there, we don't have to deliberately focus on certain points of grammar. If this corollary is correct, it means the end of grammatically based language teaching.

Before discussing this, it is important to emphasize that grammatical accuracy is an important goal. What we are discussing is how to attain this goal. I am arguing that comprehensible input is a better way of developing grammatical accuracy than direct instruction in grammar.

We all remember grammatically based classes. Students focus on one rule at a time, the idea being to "master" one rule and then move on to the next. It simply doesn't work. I will discuss four problems with the grammatically based syllabus, problems that I think are unsolvable for the grammatical syllabus, but that comprehensible input solves with ease.

1. What if a student misses class one day? If the class is based on grammar, the student has missed "the rule of the day." If the class is based on comprehensible input, however, there is no problem. Every class will contain a rich supply of grammar and vocabulary, and there will be plenty of chances for the student to get comprehensible input containing $i + 1$. With grammar-based teaching, the student gets only one chance, unless review is constant and extensive. With comprehensible input, there are many many chances.

2. Even though we all acquire language in the same way, there is individual variation in rate of acquisition. Some students in a class will progress faster than others. Individual variation in rate is especially likely in second-language classes; some students get more input outside of class than others. If the "rule of the day" is the past tense, some students may have already acquired it, and some may be nowhere

near ready. With comprehensible input, everybody is covered, even though $i + 1$ may be different for different students. We need not know exactly where each student is in his or her developmental path; all we need to do is to provide a great deal of comprehensible input.

3. In order to teach grammar, a teacher has to know grammar, and this is a task that is getting harder every day. With each new discovery, with each new grammatical rule, each new rule of sociolinguistic competence, the curriculum gets more and more complex. And it will never end. But if instruction is based on comprehensible input, this problem disappears. If comprehensible input is plentiful, students will absorb the rules teachers and good authors use, whether teachers consciously know the rules or not, whether linguists have discovered them or not.

4. The final problem with grammar teaching is the most serious: It's boring. It is very hard to say things that are interesting and comprehensible when your hidden agenda is the relative clause. But if instruction is based on comprehensible input, all we need to do is to present messages that are interesting and comprehensible, and grammar will take care of itself. As most teachers know, this task is difficult enough.

We can now return to the third "amazing fact" about the natural order hypothesis. With comprehensible input–based language teaching the syllabus is not based on the natural order. If the arguments presented in this section are correct, the syllabus is not based on any grammatical order. Rather, students will acquire the language in a natural order as a result of getting comprehensible input.

The Affective Filter Hypothesis

The affective filter hypothesis claims that affective variables do not impact language acquisition directly but prevent input from reaching what Chomsky has called the "language acquisition device," the part of the brain responsible for language acquisition. If the acquirer is anxious, has low self-esteem, does not consider himself or herself to be a potential member of the group that speaks the language (see Smith 1988 for discussion of this last factor), he or she may understand the input, but it will not reach the language acquisition device. A block, the affective filter, will keep it out. The presence of the affective filter explains how two students can receive the same (comprehensible) input, yet one makes progress while the other does not. One student is open to the input while the other is not.

Part 2: Applications

Do We Need Language Classes?

Most people don't think that language classes are necessary. Most people would say that the best way to acquire another language is to go to the country where it is spoken. But for beginners, this is bad advice. If a beginner goes to the country, he or she will only encounter a great deal of incomprehensible input. Beginners are much better off in well-taught language classes. Good language classes will give the beginner the comprehensible input that the outside world will supply only very reluctantly. A beginner can get more comprehensible input in one session of a well-taught language class than from several days of being in the country.

The goal of the language classes is to bring the beginner to the point where he or she can go to the country and obtain comprehensible input. It is important to point out that the goal of the language classes is not to bring students to the highest levels of competence. The goal is to bring students to the intermediate level. When foreign-language students reach this level they can go to the country and continue to improve on their own; they can have conversations and read at least some authentic texts. When second-language students reach this stage, they can begin to get at least some comprehensible input from the environment and from the "mainstream" in school. They will not, however, be perfect.

For those who think this is too humble a goal, for those who expect perfection from language pedagogy, I should point out that the profession has not yet been particularly successful at this more modest goal. Moreover, this modest goal is consistent with a general philosophy of education that most of us subscribe to. After completing one's basic education, one is not a master; true mastery comes only after years of experience. Education is, rather, a launching pad: it prepares us to begin our profession, and we expect to grow and improve as we practice our profession. The idea applies to the beginning-level language class.

The Beginning Level

At the beginning level, there are several methods that work. They are consistent with the underlying theory outlined here, and the research confirms that they work. Here is what they have in common:

1. The classroom hour is filled with aural comprehensible input. Teachers help make input comprehensible in several ways: First, they provide context in the form of pictures and realia, and in the use of movement. In the powerful Total Physical Response (TPR) method, language is taught using commands. The teacher gives the command, models the movement, and the student performs the action. Students are not asked to speak, only to try to understand and obey the command. The teacher's modeling of the movement is the context that helps make the command comprehensible.

2. In addition, teachers help make input comprehensible by modifying their speech. The adjustments they make, however, are not rigidly imposed. Rather, teachers naturally tend to talk a little slower and use somewhat less complex language as they try to make themselves understood.

3. The syllabus is organized. A comprehensible input–based method does not mean that we simply go in and talk to students. Comprehensible input–based classes have lesson plans and syllabi, but the syllabi are not based on points of grammar. Rather, they are based on activities (e.g., games, discussions of topics of interest, projects) that students at that level and with that background will find interesting

and comprehensible (they can be "enterprises," as discussed in Chapter 4). Thus, an activity that might work for a university-level French class in Boston may not work for an elementary school EFL class in Taiwan. Brown and Palmer (1988) suggest some very interesting activities for beginning language students that are useful for a wide range of students: magic tricks, simple scientific experiments, playing darts, playing card games, learning to do a headstand, etc. Brown and Palmer's suggestions illustrate the freedom comprehensible input teachers have. All that is required is that the activity be interesting and comprehensible. There is no requirement that the activity provide practice with a particular grammatical structure. As corollary 2 to the input hypothesis stated, given enough comprehensible input, $i + 1$ is automatically provided.

4. Demands for output are low and students are not forced to speak until they feel ready. Of course, students are not forbidden from speaking; in fact, they are warmly encouraged to speak. As noted earlier, speaking per se does not cause language acquisition, but it can invite others to talk to you, and it can lower the affective filter by making the speaker feel more like a member of the group that speaks the language.

    In comprehensible input–based methods, beginning students are able to participate in activities while saying nothing, or very little. Complete sentences are not required, and errors are not corrected. Theory predicts that grammatical accuracy is a result of comprehensible input, not output and correction, a prediction supported by the research showing disappointing results for error correction (Krashen 1981, 1994a; Truscott 1996).

5. Grammar is included, but only for older students (high school age and older), not for children. In the Natural Approach at the college level (Krashen and Terrell 1983), grammar is done as homework. Grammar is included for two reasons: First, to satisfy the curiosity some students have about the structure of language—in other words, as basic linguistics, a subject that is interesting and valuable. Second, consciously learned knowledge of grammar can be used to fill in some of the gaps left by incomplete acquisition (see "The Monitor Hypothesis," above).

As noted earlier, acquisition will give us nearly all of a language, but not 100 percent. Writing that will be read by other people must be 100 percent accurate. Comprehensible input–based methodology for older students therefore provides for the conscious learning of rules that many people, despite extensive listening and reading, may not acquire. Also as noted earlier, such rules should be used when they do not interfere with communication, as in the editing stage of composing. It is not expected that rules learned in the grammar activities will be available for spontaneous use in conversation. There is no expectation, in other words, that learned grammar rules will become acquired.

Method Comparisons: Comprehensible Input Versus Skill-Building

Comprehensible input–based methods have done very well in the published, professional research literature. When tests are communicative, students in these classes typically do considerably better than those in traditional, grammar-based classes.

Table 1–1
TPR Versus Traditional Instruction

LISTENING

	n	TPR	n	TRAD
Grade 5	51	35.3		
Grade 6	166	43.4		
Grades 7–8	50	45.5	17	51.32
Grade 9			22	38.4

READING

	n	TPR	n	TRAD
Grade 5	51	33.6		
Grade 6	166	45.1		
Grades 7–8	50	50.1	17	51.2
Grade 9			47	36.5

Note: TPR had 20 hours of instruction, comparisons had
100 hours (grade 9) or 200 hours (grades 7–8)
(*Source*: Asher 1977)

When grammar tests are used, there is either no difference, or comprehensible input students are slightly better. I present here a few samples of the research (see also Krashen 1981, 1982, 1994a).

Asher has published a number of studies in which TPR was compared to traditional foreign-language methodology. Table 1–1 presents data from Asher (1977). Subjects were public school children in the United States studying Spanish as a foreign language. TPR students had received only twenty hours of instruction in TPR, while comparison, traditionally taught children had received one hundred hours (ninth graders) or two hundred hours (combined seventh- and eighth-grade classes). Traditional methodology included students' repeating what instructors said, the use of translation to communicate meaning, and formal instruction in reading and writing, "emphasizing Spanish grammar" (1044). The listening measure included seventy items and asked students to listen to a sentence and view a picture at the same time, and judge whether the sentence was true, false, or incomprehensible. The reading test was identical, except that subjects read the sentence.

The results were astounding. Sixth graders with only twenty hours of TPR Spanish actually outperformed ninth graders with five times as much exposure to Spanish ($d = 0.58$ for listening comprehension, $d = 1.05$ for reading comprehension). The combined seventh and eighth graders who did TPR also did better than the ninth-grade comparisons ($d = 0.81$ for listening comprehension, $d = 1.18$ for reading).[1] Comparisons with two hundred hours of instruction outperformed the TPR students, but recall that they had ten times as much exposure to Spanish!

This is only one of many studies showing the superiority of TPR over traditional approaches. In Asher, Kusudo and de la Torre (1974) TPR students after

Table 1–2

Comparison of Traditional and Comprehensible Input Methodology

1986	TRAD	CI	p
n	18	7	
LC	1.47	1.57	ns
Reading	1.44	1.79	$< .05$
Speaking	1.56	1.21	$< .10$
1987	**TRAD**	**CI**	p
n	23	7	
LC	1.26	1.5	$< .20$
Reading	1.41	1.64	$< .20$
Speaking	1.5	1.36	ns
1988	**TRAD**	**CI**	p
n	43	18	
LC	1.31	1.61	$< .05$
Reading	1.3	1.44	$< .20$
Speaking	1.35	1.53	$< .20$

(Two students in each section did not take the speaking test in 1989)
ns = not significant
(*Source*: Nicola 1990)

90 hours exceeded the fiftieth percentile on a standardized Spanish test designed for students who had had 150 hours of instruction. In Asher (1972), adult TPR students of German who had had only 32 hours of instruction outperformed two control groups who had traditional instruction, one that had 40 hours and another that had 80 hours.[2] Several additional replications of these results have been published (e.g. Asher 1966, 1969, 1972; Swaffer and Woodruff 1978; Wolfe and Jones 1982).

Recent Studies

Hammond (1988) compared the attainment of eight randomly selected classes of university-level Spanish who experienced a comprehensible input-based method, the Natural Approach (Krashen and Terrell 1983), with fifty-two classes that experienced "modified grammar-translation." On a grammar test given at the end of the semester, Natural Approach students were slightly better (according to my calculations, $d = 0.15$; $p < 0.07$).

Nicola (1990) compared "grammar audio-lingual" methodology to a method that focused more on comprehensible input and meaning, and less on form, for students of Arabic at the Defense Language Institute. The treatment lasted about thirty weeks and students met six hours per day, but about half the material was common to both groups. We have no details about the nature of the test, nor was it possible to

Table 1–3

Comprehensible Input vs. Grammar Emphasis

METHOD	n	MEAN	sd
Explicit grammar	72	30.5	4.29
Implicit	67	33.38	5.21

d = 0.61; perfect = 54; sd = standard deviation
(*Source*: Winitz 1996)

compute effect sizes, but it is clear from an inspection of the data that students who received more comprehensible input consistently did better on tests of listening and reading. For the first two groups studied, traditional students were better on an oral test, but CI students in the third group studied were better (see Table 1–2 on page 10).

Winitz (1996) compared the progress of college Spanish students in the United States after one semester of an "implicit grammar" approach in which the focus "was on the presentation of comprehensible input" (36). Activities were organized so that basic grammatical forms were covered, but the focus was on meaning. Students in this section were free to speak when they wished, but errors were not corrected. The explicit students followed a traditional approach, using a text that gave "explicit descriptions of grammatical rules before or after many examples of usage" (36). Table 1–3 presents the results of a test of grammaticality judgments. The test consisted of fifty-four sentences in Spanish and subjects were asked to indicate if the sentences were grammatical or ungrammatical. The implicit grammar group did better.

Nikolov and Krashen (1997) was a comparison of grammatical accuracy and fluency in two EFL classes in Pecs, Hungary, followed over seven years. The experimental class had a story-based syllabus, and a focus on content, with no formal grammar instruction and no focus on form until grade 8, the last year of the study. The comparison group followed a structural syllabus, with explicit rules, drills, and exercises. An analysis was done of accuracy and fluency in an interview situation in which students were asked to talk about themselves, describe a person they knew, a book they had read, or a film they had seen.

An analysis of nine grammatical morphemes in obligatory occasions showed that the experimental group was more fluent (3,366 obligatory occasions produced, compared to 2,742), and was slightly more accurate (87 percent correct, compared to 82 percent). The experimental group was more accurate on five of the nine items, and there was no difference on two. These results confirm that comprehensible input can produce both accuracy and fluency. In addition, after the study was complete, Nikolov maintained contact with the students: thirteen of the fifteen in the story-based class passed a form-focused proficiency examination in English at the university level, and four became English majors.

Isik's (2000) study shows that a combination of 75 percent comprehensible input and 25 percent grammar is more effective than 80 percent grammar and 20 percent communicative activities. Isik compared two groups of twenty students, low

Table 1–4
Comprehensible Input vs. Grammar Emphasis

	COMPREHENSIBLE INPUT	GRAMMAR	EFFECT SIZE
Oxford grammar test	67.6 (5.0)	45.6 (9.6)	2.87
PET: reading	22.25 (1.07)	14.5 (4.26)	2.87
PET: LC	24.9 (2.29)	17.5 (3.3)	2.66
PET: writing	19.4 (2.6)	7.5 (3.3)	4.03

PET = Preliminary English Test
(*Source*: Isik 2000)

intermediates in EFL studying in Turkey in high school. The comprehensible input group devoted seven hours a week to formal grammar study. The rest of the time (twenty-two hours) was spent on TPR and communication-based activities, with minimal correction. Students in this section also read two graded readers per week. The grammar group devoted twenty-four hours per week (out of twenty-nine) to form-based activities, moving from mechanical to meaningful practice, with a focus on correct production: "... meaning was secondary and immediate correction was provided" (251). The duration of the study was thirty-six weeks, a total of about one thousand hours. Results presented in Table 1–4 show that the comprehensible input group was far superior in all tests.

My goal is this section was not to present a complete survey of method comparisons, but simply to present some sample studies, and to give readers an idea of how robust the advantage for comprehensible input–based instruction is.

The Intermediate Level: Sheltered Subject-Matter Teaching

As effective as comprehensible input–based methodology is, it is not enough. Methods such as Total Physical Response and Natural Approach provide "conversational" language. Second-language students need more: they need advanced, or "academic" language proficiency (Cummins 1981), the language of history texts, story problems in math, and the language of business, science, and politics. It is also the language of the classics. A very effective way to develop academic language is through wide reading, a topic that is discussed in the next chapter. In this chapter, I present an additional way of doing this: sheltered subject-matter teaching.

Inspired by the success of Canadian immersion programs (see, e.g., Lambert and Tucker 1972), sheltered subject-matter teaching derives from one important concept: subject-matter teaching, when it is comprehensible, is language teaching, because it provides comprehensible input. Sheltered subject-matter teaching has two important characteristics:

1. It is not for beginners and not for native speakers of the language. In sheltered classes, only intermediate second-language acquirers participate. The input will not be comprehensible for beginners. Beginners are better off in TPR, Natural,

Approach, and related methods. When we allow native speakers of the language into the class, there is a real danger that the input will no longer be comprehensible for the second-language acquirers. When all students are more or less in the same linguistic boat, it is easier for the teacher to make sure the input is comprehensible.

2. In sheltered classes, students and teachers are focused on subject matter, not language. This emphasis on meaning, and not form, results in more comprehensible input, and thus more language acquisition. Sheltered subject-matter classes are, thus, not "ESL math" or "ESL history" but are "math" and "history."

Research on sheltered subject-matter teaching

Research on sheltered subject-matter teaching has shown that students in these classes acquire considerable amounts of the second language, doing at least as well as students in regular intermediate language classes, and they also learn an impressive amount of subject matter. Thus, sheltered teaching is very time-efficient; students get both language and subject matter at the same time. Also, sheltered subject-matter teaching provides exposure to academic language. I present here two examples; for others, see Krashen (1991).

The first study done with adult students on sheltered subject-matter teaching showed that university students at the University of Ottawa could learn both psychology and make progress in a second language at the same time (Edwards, Wesche, Krashen, Clement and Kruidenier 1985; Hauptman, Wesche, and Ready 1988). Participants, who were volunteers, had already studied one semester of college psychology in their first language (English or French), and had at least low intermediate knowledge of the second language (French or English). The sheltered course was second-semester psychology (in Hauptman et al., one experimental group did sheltered psychology for two semesters), and was supplemented by a half-hour weekly session with a language teacher, who did no direct grammar teaching, but focused on comprehension of content and "developing strategies for effective reading and class interventions" (Hauptman et al., 445). In general, subjects made progress in second-language acquisition equivalent to students in regular second-language classes, and acquired subject matter just as well as students who took the same course in their first language.

Lafayette and Buscaglia (1985) reported that fourth-semester university-level students of French who studied French civilization and culture did just as well as a traditional fourth-semester class on several measures of French proficiency (listening and reading), and made better gains on a speaking test. Comparisons were slightly better on a grammar test, but more than 20 percent of the items on this test dealt with the subjunctive, a late-acquired aspect of grammar that was emphasized in the traditional class.

Continuation Studies

Indirect evidence for the hypothesis that comprehensible input–based methods are effective are findings showing that more students in these classes continue on and do additional study more than students in traditional classes. Swaffer and Woodruff (1978) reported that enrollment in second-semester German classes increased after students experienced a comprehension-based first-semester course. The attrition rate between the first and second semesters under traditional instruction was 45 percent and 47 percent in the two years studied. After comprehension-based instruction, attrition dropped to 28 percent and 22 percent in two consecutive years.

Cononelos (cited in Sternfeld 1992) compared students who had completed five quarters of traditional skill-based foreign-language instruction (German) with students at the same university who had completed five quarters of an "immersion/multiliteracy" program, which was sheltered subject-matter teaching focusing on culture and civilization. Of 109 traditional students, only 4 went on to take more advanced courses in the foreign language. In contrast, 9 out of 22 former sheltered students went on to higher levels; according to my calculations, this difference is highly significant (Fisher Test, $p < .0001$). While immersion/multiliteracy students made up only 17 percent of the fifth-quarter students surveyed, "they accounted for fully 69 % of the students enrolled in upper division courses" (Sternfeld 1992, 435). Similarly, in Lafayette and Buscaglia (1985), discussed above, more students from the sheltered fourth-semester French class said they intended to enroll for advanced French (50 percent, compared to 36 percent of the comparison students), and 94 percent said the course was more interesting than other French courses they had taken at the same university.

In this chapter I reviewed some of the basics of language acquisition theory and some general applications. The next chapter discusses a powerful means of helping students move to more advanced levels of proficiency, one that has been nearly completely neglected: free voluntary reading.

Notes

1. d is a measure of effect size. If $d = 1.0$, this indicates an advantage of one standard deviation for the experimental group. Effect sizes were calculated by the author from statistics presented in the original paper, usually from means and standard deviations, but sometimes from values of t and F.

2. Baretta (1986) noted that in this study the same activity was used as a class activity as well as a posttest, which, he suggests, explains why TPR students in German did better than controls. Baretta also noted that TPR and control students performed equally on a reading comprehension test. Baretta does not report Asher in full. First, TPR students in Asher (1972) also did better than controls on a listening test that did not include the repeated activities. In addition, controls had 35 percent more hours' exposure to German and had much more emphasis on reading and writing. Baretta also points out a reporting error in Krashen (1982). I had claimed that in Asher (1972) TPR students with thirty-two hours of exposure did as well as controls with one hundred fifty hours of exposure to German. Baretta points out that this was "quite simply not the case" (433). As noted here, however, TPR students still did spectacularly well in this and other studies.

2

Free Voluntary Reading: Still a Very Good Idea

ree voluntary reading may be the most powerful tool we have in language education. In fact, it appears to be too good to be true. It is an effective way of
increasing literacy and language development, with a strong impact on reading
comprehension, vocabulary, grammar, and writing. It is also very pleasant. In fact, it
is more than pleasant: it is extremely enjoyable. Free reading may also be an important
part of the solution to two related problems: making the transition from the elementary level to authentic language use, and from "conversational" language ability to
"academic" language ability.

Free voluntary reading works, I propose, because it is a form of comprehensible
input delivered in a low-anxiety situation (Krashen 1994a; Chapter 1 of this volume).
In this chapter, I briefly review the evidence for free reading, some practical issues, and,
even though it is hardly necessarily, evidence showing that free reading is enjoyable.

Research on Free Reading

Correlational Studies

Studies in both second- and foreign-language acquisition confirm that those who read
more do better on a wide variety of tests. I include here some recent studies in foreign-
and second-language acquisition (see Krashen 1993b for earlier studies). In Stokes,
Krashen, and Kartchner (1998), students of Spanish as a foreign language in the United
States were tested on their knowledge of the subjunctive on a test that attempted to
probe acquired competence (in the results presented below, only subjects who were
not aware that the subjunctive was the focus of the test were included). Formal study
was not a predictor of subjunctive competence, nor was length of residence in a
Spanish-speaking country. Stokes, Krashen, and Kartchner also asked subjects about
the quality of instruction they had had specifically in the subjunctive. This variable
also failed to predict performance on the subjunctive test. The amount of free reading
in Spanish, however, was a clear predictor (Table 2–1).

Lee, Krashen, and Gribbons (1996) reported that for international students in
the United States, the amount of free reading reported (number of years subjects
read newspapers, news magazines, popular magazines, fiction, and nonfiction) was a

Table 2–1
Predictors of Performance on the Subjunctive in Spanish
(Multiple Regression Analysis)

Predictor	beta	t	p
Formal study	0.0518	0.36	0.718
Length of residence	0.0505	0.35	0.726
Amount of reading	0.3222	2.19	0.034
Subj study	0.0454	0.31	0.757

$r2 = .12, p = .128$
(*Source*: Stokes, Krashen, and Kartchner 1998)

significant predictor of the ability to translate and judge the grammaticality of complex grammatical constructions in English (restrictive relative clauses). The amount of formal study and length of residence in the United States were not significant predictors. Results for the grammaticality judgment task are presented in Table 2–2 (translation results were similar).

Constantino, Lee, Cho, and Krashen (1997) reported that the amount of free reading international students living in the United States said they did before taking the Test of English as a Foreign Language (TOEFL) was an excellent predictor of their score on this examination (Table 2–3). In this study, formal study and length of residence were also significant (and independent) predictors.

Case Histories

Cho and Krashen (1994) demonstrated substantial and obvious growth in vocabulary in English as a second language in adult English acquirers who were encouraged to read novels in the Sweet Valley High series. Subjects had had some instruction in English as a second or foreign language (heavily grammar based), and began with the Sweet Valley Kids (second-grade level) series, moving eventually to Sweet Twins (fourth-grade level) and to Sweet Valley High (fifth- and sixth-grade level).

Table 2–2
Grammaticality Judgment Test (Multiple Regression Analysis)

Predictor	beta	t	p
Amount of reading	0.516	3.98	0.0002
Formal study	0.072	0.57	0.568
Length of residence	0.052	0.4	0.69

$r2 = .29, p < .05$
(*Source*: Lee, Krashen, and Gribbons 1996)

Table 2–3
Predictors of Performance on the TOEFL Test (Multiple Regression Analysis)

Predictor	beta	t	p
Free reading/books	0.41	3.422	0.002
English study/home	0.48	3.72	0.001
LOR/US	0.42	3.243	0.003

r2 = .45
(*Source*: Constantino et al. 1997)

They showed clear gains in vocabulary, and vastly increased confidence in speaking English.

Segal (1997) describes the case of L., a seventeen-year-old eleventh-grade student in Israel. L. speaks English at home with her parents, who are from South Africa, but had serious problems in English writing, especially in spelling, vocabulary, and writing style. Segal, L.'s teacher in grade 10, tried a variety of approaches:

> Error correction proved a total failure. L. tried correcting her own mistakes, tried process writing, and tried just copying words correctly in her notebook. Nothing worked. L.'s compositions were poorly expressed and her vocabulary was weak. We conferenced together over format and discussed ideas before writing. We made little progress. I gave L. a list of five useful words to spell each week for six weeks and tested her in an unthreatening way during recess. L. performed well in the tests in the beginning, but by the end of six weeks she reverted to misspelling the words she had previously spelt correctly.

In addition, L.'s mother got her a private tutor, but there was little improvement.

Segal also taught L. in grade 11. At the beginning of the year, she assigned an essay: "When I came to L.'s composition I stopped still. Before me was an almost perfect essay. There were no spelling mistakes. The paragraphs were clearly marked. Her ideas were well put and she made good sense. Her vocabulary had improved. I was amazed but at the same time uneasy . . ." Segal discovered the reason for L.'s improvement: She had become a reader over the summer. L. told her, "I never read much before but this summer I went to the library and I started reading and I just couldn't stop." L.'s performance in grade 11 in English was consistently excellent and her reading habit has continued.

Cohen (1997) attended an English-language medium school in her native Turkey, beginning at age twelve. The first two years were devoted to intensive English study, and Cohen reports that after only two months, she started to read in English, "as many books in English as I could get hold of. I had a rich, ready-made library of English books at home . . . I became a member of the local British Council's library and occasionally purchased English books in bookstores . . . By the first year of middle school I had become an avid reader of English."

Her reading, however, led to an "unpleasant incident" in middle school: "I had a new English teacher who assigned us two compositions for homework. She returned them to me ungraded, furious. She wanted to know who had helped me write them. They were my personal work. I had not even used the dictionary. She would not believe me. She pointed at a few underlined sentences and some vocabulary and asked me how I knew them; they were well beyond the level of the class. I had not even participated much in class. I was devastated. There and then and many years later I could not explain how I knew them. I just did."

In-School Free Reading

In-school free reading studies include evaluations of several kinds of programs: In sustained silent reading, students read whatever they please (within reason) for a short time each day and there is no accountability required. In extensive reading programs, a small amount of accountability is included; for example, a short description of what was read. In self-selected reading programs, the entire class period is devoted to reading, and occasional teacher-student conferences are scheduled.

I have reviewed the available research on in-school free reading in several places (Krashen 1993b, 2001). In my most recent summary (Krashen 2001), I found that students who participated in these programs did as well or better than comparison students in traditional language arts or second-language programs on tests of reading comprehension in fifty-one out of fifty-four comparisons. The results were even more impressive when one considers only studies lasting one academic year or longer: in eight out of ten cases, participants in in-school reading programs outperformed comparisons and in two cases there was no difference.

The National Reading Panel (NRP), supported by the U.S. Government, also reviewed studies of in-school reading, and reached the startling conclusion that there is no clear evidence supporting this practice. They were, however, able to find only fourteen comparisons, all lasting less than one academic year, between students in in-school free reading programs and comparison children, devoting only 6 pages of their massive report to this topic (as compared to approximately 120 pages devoted to research on phonemic awareness and phonics). Interestingly, in-school reading did not fare badly even in the limited analysis done by the NRP, with in-school readers doing better in four cases, and never doing worse. Note that even a finding of "no difference" suggests that free reading is just as good as traditional instruction, an important theoretical and practical point. Because free reading is so much more pleasant than regular instruction (see below), and because it provides readers with valuable information, a finding of no difference provides strong evidence in favor of free reading in classrooms.

I have also argued (Krashen 2001) that the NRP not only missed many, many studies, they also misinterpreted some of the ones they included. I present here a discussion of recent studies that have particular relevance to the EFL situation.

In Elley and Mangubhai (1983), fourth- and fifth-grade students of English as a foreign language were divided into three groups for their thirty-minute daily English class. One group had traditional audio-lingual method instruction, a second did only

Table 2–4
In-School Reading in South Africa: Reading Comprehension Results

PROVINCE	STD 3		STD 4		STD 5	
	Read	Nonread	Read	Nonread	Read	Nonread
Eastern Cape	32.5	25.6	44.0	32.5	58.1	39.0
Western Cape	36.2	30.2	40.4	34.3	53.0	40.4
Free State	32.3	30.1	44.3	37.1	47.2	40.5
Natal	39.5	28.3	47.0	32.3	63.1	35.1

STD = standard
STD 3 = grade 4
(*Source*: Elley 1998)

free reading, while a third did "shared reading." Shared reading " . . . is a method of sharing a good book with a class, several times, in such a way that the students are read to by the teacher, as in a bedtime story. They then talk about the book, they read it together, they act out the story, they draw parts of it and write their own caption, they rewrite the story with different characters or events . . ." (Elley 1998, 1–2). After two years, the free-reading group and the shared-reading group were far superior to the traditional group in tests of reading comprehension, writing, and grammar. Similar results were obtained by Elley (1991) in a large-scale study of second-language acquirers, ages six through nine, in Singapore.

Elley's recent data (Elley 1998) comes from South Africa and Sri Lanka. In all cases, children who were encouraged to read for pleasure outperformed traditionally taught students on standardized tests of reading comprehension and on other measures of literacy. Table 2–4 presents the data from South Africa. In this study, EFL students who lived in print-poor environments were given access to sets of sixty high-interest books, which were placed in classrooms, with another sixty made available in sets of six identical titles. The books were used for read-alouds by the teacher, for shared reading, and for silent reading. Table 2–4 presents data from different provinces; in every case the readers outperformed those in comparison classes, and the gap widened with each year of reading.

Mason (Mason and Krashen 1997) developed a version of extensive reading for university EFL students in Japan in which students do self-selected reading of pedagogical readers as well as easy authentic reading. Accountability was present but minimal; students only had to write a short "appreciation" of what they had read. In three separate studies, Mason found that extensive readers made greater gains than comparison students who participated in traditional form-based EFL classes. Table 2–5 presents the details of the three studies in the form of effect sizes comparing the extensive readers to the traditionally taught students.

Lao and Krashen (2000) compared progress in reading over one semester between university-level EFL students in Hong Kong who participated in a popular-literature class that emphasized reading for content and enjoyment, including some

Table 2–5

Extensive Reading Compared to Traditional Methods of Teaching EFL

STUDY	SUBJECTS	DURATION	MEASURE	RESULTS	EFFECT SIZE
1	4-year college	1 sem	Cloze test	ER > trad.	0.702
2a	4-year college	1 yr	Cloze test	ER > trad.	1.11
2b	2-year college	1 yr	Cloze test	ER > trad.	1.47
3	4-year college	1 yr	Cloze test	ER = cloze[a]	0.244
	(reactions		RC	ER > cloze[a]	0.609
	written in				
	Japanese)				
	4-year college		Cloze test	ER > cloze[a]	0.63
	(reactions written		RC	ER > cloze[a]	0.48
	in English)				

RC = reading comprehension; ER = extensive reading
[a]Cloze = traditional instruction with emphasis on cloze exercises
Effect size calculation = (mean of ER group − mean of traditional)/pooled standard deviation.
(*Source*: Mason and Krashen 1997)

self-selected reading, and students in a traditional academic skills class. Application of statistical tests, including those that accounted for pretest differences, confirmed that the superiority of the popular literature group was statistically significant. As shown in Table 2–6, the popular-literature students made better gains in vocabulary and reading rate and, at the end of the semester, clearly felt that what they had learned in the course would help them in their other university courses.[1]

Shin (2001) examined the impact of a six-week self-selected reading experience among two hundred sixth- and seventh-graders who had to attend summer school because of low reading proficiency. Students attended class four hours per day; during this time, approximately two hours were devoted to sustained silent reading, including twenty-five minutes in the school library. The district invested $25 per student on popular paperbacks and magazines, with most books purchased from the Goosebumps series. In addition, about forty-five minutes per day were devoted to reading and discussing novels such as *Holes* and *The Island of the Blue Dolphins*. Comparison children (*n* = 160) followed a standard language arts curriculum during the summer. Attrition was high for both groups but similar (class size dropped from 20 to 14.3 among readers, and from 20 to 13.2 among comparisons) as was the percentage of limited English proficient children (31 percent in the reading group, 27 percent in the comparison group). The readers gained approximately five months on the Altos test of reading comprehension and vocabulary over the six-week period, while comparisons declined. On the Nelson-Denny reading comprehension test, the summer readers grew a spectacular 1.3 years (from grade 4.0 to grade 5.4). On the vocabulary section, however, the groups showed equivalent gains.

Table 2–6
Popular Literature vs. Traditional Instruction

	VOCABULARY		READING RATE		HELP IN OTHER COURSES		
	Pre	Post	Pre	Post	Yes	No	Don't know
Popular literature	7	8	10.7	17.3	88	3	
Traditional	5.1	5.2	7.4	7.9	12	22	5

scores in grade level equivalents
(*Source*: Lao and Krashen 2000)

The Author Recognition Test: A Methodological Breakthrough

Stanovich, in a series of studies, has verified the value of a simple procedure for studying the impact of reading. In the author recognition test, subjects simply indicate whether they recognize the names of authors on a list. For speakers of English as a first language, scores on the author recognition test have been shown to correlate substantially with measures of vocabulary (West and Stanovich 1991; West, Stanovich, and Mitchell 1993; Lee, Krashen, and Tse 1997), reading comprehension (Cipielewski and Stanovich 1990; Stanovich and West 1989) and spelling (Cunningham and Stanovich 1990). These results have been confirmed using other first languages as well: Significant correlations have been reported between performance on an author recognition test and writing performance in Chinese (Lee and Krashen 1996), and Korean (Kim and Krashen 1998a), and between author recognition test performance and vocabulary development in Spanish (Rodrigo, McQuillan, and Krashen 1996).

Those who report reading more also do better on the author recognition test. This is true for English speakers (Stanovich and West 1989; Allen, Cipielewski, and Stanovich 1992), Korean speakers (Kim and Krashen 1998a), Chinese speakers (Lee and Krashen 1996), and Spanish speakers (Rodrigo, McQuillan, and Krashen 1996). One study also reported a positive correlation between performance on the author recognition test and the amount of reading subjects were observed doing. West, Stanovich, and Mitchell (1993) observed airport passengers waiting for flights and classified them as either readers (those who were observed to be reading for at least ten continuous minutes) or nonreaders. Readers did significantly better on an author recognition test as well as on a vocabulary recognition test.

Only one study thus far has examined the performance of foreign language students on the author recognition test. Kim and Krashen (1998b) reported that for high school students of English as a foreign language, performance on an English author recognition test was a good predictor of performance on an English vocabulary test. In addition, those who reported more free reading in English also tended to do better on the author recognition test.

Table 2–7
Common and Uncommon Words in Speech and Writing

	FREQUENT WORDS	RARE WORDS
Adults talking to children	95.6	9.9
Adults talking to adults (college grads)	93.9	17.3
Prime-time TV: adult	94.0	22.7
Children's books	92.3	30.9
Comic books	88.6	53.5
Books	88.4	52.7
Popular magazines	85.0	65.7
Newspapers	84.3	68.3
Abstracts of scientific papers	70.3	128.2

frequent words = percentage of text from most frequent 1,000 words
rare words = number of rare words (not in most common 10,000) per 1,000 tokens.
(*Source*: Hayes and Ahrens 1988)

In addition to providing confirmation of the relation between recreational reading and language development, the author recognition test and similar measures (magazine recognition test, title recognition test) promise to simplify work in this area.

Light Reading As a Bridge

Of course, a great deal of free reading will be "light reading." Research by Hayes and Ahrens (1988) supports the idea that lighter reading can prepare readers for heavier reading. According to their findings, it is highly unlikely that much educated vocabulary comes from conversation or television. Hayes and Ahrens found that the frequency of less-common words in ordinary conversation, whether adult-to-child or adult-to-adult, was much lower than in even the "lightest" reading. About 95 percent of the words used in conversation and television are from the most frequent 5,000. Printed texts include far more uncommon words, leading Hayes and Ahrens to the conclusion that the development of lexical knowledge beyond basic words "requires literacy and extensive reading across a broad range of subjects" (409). Table 2–7 presents some of their data, including two of the three measures they used for word frequency. Note that light reading (comics, novels, other adult books, and magazines), although somewhat closer to conversation, occupies a position between conversation and abstracts of scientific papers.[2]

Other Advantages of Reading

In Krashen (1994b), I proposed the pleasure hypothesis: Pedagogical activities that promote language acquisition are enjoyable, and those that do not are not enjoyable (and may even be painful). Of course, just because an activity is enjoyable does not mean it is good for language acquisition; some activities may be very enjoyable but may not help at all. Enjoyment is no guarantee of effectiveness. It is, however, interesting that there is strong evidence that free voluntary reading is very enjoyable.

The evidence includes work by Csikszentmihalyi (1991), who introduced the concept of flow. Flow is the state people reach when they are deeply but effortlessly involved in an activity. In flow, the concerns of everyday life and even the sense of self disappear—our sense of time is altered and nothing but the activity itself seems to matter. Crosscultural studies indicate that flow is easily recognized by members of widely different cultures and groups. For example, members of Japanese motorcycle gangs experience flow when riding (Sato 1992) and rock climbers experience flow when climbing (Massimini, Csikszentmihalyi, and Della Fave 1992).

Of special interest is the finding that reading "is currently perhaps the most often mentioned flow activity in the world" (Csikszentmihalyi 1991, 117). This finding is consistent with reports of individual pleasure readers. A resident in Walse in Northern Italy said that when he reads, "I immediately immerse myself in the reading and the problems I usually worry about disappear" (Massimini, Csikszentmihalyi, and Della Fave 1992, 68). One of Nell's subjects reported that "reading removes me . . . from the . . . irritations of living . . . for the few hours a day I read 'trash' I escape the cares of those around me, as well as escaping my own cares and dissatisfactions . . ." (Nell 1988, 240). W. Somerset Maugham, quoted in Nell (1988), had similar comments: "Conversation after a time bores me, games tire me, and my own thoughts, which we are told are the unfailing resource of a sensible man, have a tendency to run dry. Then I fly to my book as the opium-smoker to his pipe . . ." (232).

Nell provided interesting evidence showing why bedtime reading is so pleasant. Pleasure readers were asked to read a book of their own choice while their heart rate, muscle activity, skin potential, and respiration rate were measured; level of arousal while reading was compared to arousal during other activities, such as relaxing with eyes shut, listening to white noise, doing mental arithmetic, and doing visualization activities. Nell found that during reading, arousal was increased, as compared to relaxation with eyes shut, but a clear decline in arousal was recorded in the period just after reading, which for some measures reached a level below the baselines (eyes-shut) condition. In other words, bedtime reading is arousing, but then it relaxes you. Consistent with these findings are Nell's results showing that bedtime reading is popular. Of twenty-six pleasure readers he interviewed, thirteen read in bed every night and eleven "almost every night" or "most nights" (1988, 250).

Free reading has additional benefits. Lee and Krashen (1997) proposed that those who read more have less "writing apprehension" because of their superior command of the written language. They reported a modest but positive correlation between the amount of reading done and scores on a writing apprehension questionniare for Taiwanese high school students. The modest size of the correlation ($r = .21$) may be because other factors affect writing apprehension, such as mastery of the composing process. It is consistent, however, with reports that those with less writing apprehension enjoy reading more (Daly and Wilson 1983). Free reading is also an excellent source of knowledge: those who read more, know more (see discussion in Chapter 3;

e.g., Ravitch and Finn 1987; Schaefer and Anastasi 1968; Simonton 1988; Stanovich, West, and Harrison 1995).

Motivating Students to Read

If reading is so enjoyable, do we have to worry about motivating students to read? I think we do, but the task is much simpler than we thought. There is good evidence that rewards and incentives play no role in increasing the amount of reading done nor does it impact gains in reading comprehension (McQuillan 1997). The simpler solution is to provide students with access to plenty of interesting and comprehensible reading material and also provide some time for them to read. There is evidence that this works.

The Impact of Reading Itself

Those who participate in in-school free reading programs are motivated to read more (Pilgreen and Krashen 1993). Greaney and Clarke (1973), in fact, reported that children who participated in a sustained silent reading program reported reading more than comparison students six years after the program ended. Tse (1996) describes the case of Joyce, an adult ESL student in the United States who did not view reading as a leisure activity and had never read a book in English before coming to the United States. After participating in an extensive reading class, her attitude toward reading changed dramatically, and she continued to read after the end of the course, and she recommended that her husband take the same class, rather than a traditional class.

The Impact of One Trip to the Library

Ramos (Ramos and Krashen 1998) taught in an elementary school that had an inadequate school library. He and his fellow teachers organized a field trip for their second-grade students to a nearby public library, at a time when the library was closed to the public and the librarian was available to help and interact with the teachers and children. Ramos documented a clear and dramatic growth in interest in reading among the children after this visit. Cho and Krashen (2002) documented a clear increase in interest in reading and in promoting pleasure reading among teachers after one exposure to interesting and comprehensible children's literature.

The Impact of One Positive Reading Experience

Jim Trelease (2001) has suggested that one positive experience with reading can do the job, one "home run" experience. Two recent studies have confirmed that a surprising percentage of elementary school children report that they did indeed have one very positive experience with reading that got them interested in reading (Von Sprecken, Kim, and Krashen 2000; Kim and Krashen 2000). In both cases, children reported a wide variety of home run books, which strongly suggests that readers should have exposure to a rich variety of reading material.

There are several ways of helping ensure that a home run experience takes place. The best way is to make sure interesting reading is available, reading that students really want to do. Simply recommending books is an obvious step. Others include read-alouds (Trelease 2001), modeling reading (e.g., reading while children are reading during sustained silent reading time; see Wheldall and Entwhistle 1988 for evidence), and interesting book discussions (the core of language arts) as well as providing time to read. The time issue is an important one: there is evidence that interest in reading remains strong as students get older, but the pressures of school, and sometimes work, result in their having less time to read (Krashen and Von Sprecken 2002).

Providing Time to Read

Simply providing time to read results in reading. Von Sprecken and Krashen (1998) observed sustained silent reading (SSR) sessions in a middle school in the middle of the school year and reported that 90 percent of the students were reading. More reading tended to take place in those classrooms in which more books were available in the classroom library, in which teachers also read while students read, in which students were not required to bring their own books, and in which teachers made deliberate efforts to promote certain books. In one of the eleven classes observed, there were few books, no modeling of reading, no promotion of books, and students had to bring their own books. Nevertheless, 80 percent of the students in this class were observed to be reading during SSR.

Cohen (1999) unobtrusively observed 120 eighth-grade students during SSR time over a two-week period, and found that 94 percent were reading during SSR. She noted that enthusiasm for sustained silent reading was not high at the beginning of the school year, but increased after one or two months.

Herda and Ramos (2001) reported that 63 percent of students in SSR sessions in grades 1 through 12 were actively reading; in grades 1 through 5, the percentages were much higher, ranging from 76 percent to 100 percent. In the upper grades, students were given the option of studying or pleasure reading, and a substantial percentage took advantage of the study option. Nevertheless, a surprising percentage were reading for pleasure, ranging from 29 percent in grade 12 to 65 percent in grade nine. Overall, 21 percent of the sample were studying during SSR time and only 17 percent were neither reading nor studying.

Some Innovations

Handcrafted Books

A problem with free reading in the second- and foreign-language situation is that it is hard to find texts that are both interesting and comprehensible; the beginning student will find authentic texts too difficult. There are two solutions to this problem. One is simply to find the best pedagogic readers and make them available for free voluntary reading. A second is a recent innovation called "Handcrafted Books" (Dupuy and McQuillan 1997). Handcrafted Books are written by intermediate students, corrected by the teacher, and are to be read by beginners. Writers are instructed not to look up words while writing; if intermediate students don't know a word, the chances are good that beginners won't know it either. Handcrafted Books thus have a good chance of being interesting and comprehensible; they are written by peers who are slightly more advanced than the readers.

Sheltered Popular Literature

A very useful adjunct to sustained silent reading is a class on popular literature. Even foreign-language students who are well read in their first language may not be aware of the options for pleasure reading in the second language. Sheltered popular literature exposes students to the different kinds of light but authentic reading available, moving from comics and magazines to novels. Such a course is taught as literature; that is, with discussion of the values expressed in the reading as well as the insights they provide on the culture (for suggestions, see Dupuy, Tse, and Cook 1996). Our hope is that such a course will help students discover one or more kinds of light reading they would like to do on their own. For evidence that such a course can actually work, see Lao and Krashen (2000), discussed earlier.

If students become enthusiastic readers of any type of reading, they will progress enormously; better readers are typically "series" readers (Lamme 1974)—readers of Nancy Drew, The Black Stallion, John R. Tunis, Sweet Valley High, Goosebumps and Fear Street, and so forth. Narrow reading builds language and literacy competence rapidly, thanks to the familiar context and resulting high level of comprehensibility. In addition, acquisition of any written style should facilitate comprehension of any other; while there are differences among different types of prose, there is also substantial overlap (Biber 1988); someone who can read light fiction easily has acquired much of what is needed to read academic prose.

Conclusion

There is overwhelming evidence for recreational reading as a means of increasing second-language competence. In fact, it is now perhaps the most thoroughly investigated and best-supported technique we have in the field of second-language pedagogy. Only one aspect of recreational reading remains uninvestigated: Why isn't it used more frequently in second-language programs?

Notes

1. Sze (1999) evaluated an extensive reading program in Hong Kong. Four hundred ninety-six students from five schools, ages thirteen through fifteen, were engaged in an extensive reading project (the Hong Kong Extensive Reading Scheme [HKERS]) that had the following features:

1. Each class of forty was given one hundred books; Sze suggests that this is a large number, but it is not. It is only 2.5 books per student.

2. Students had free choice in book selection but had to answer comprehension questions; "question and answer cards" were provided with each book (64).

3. Students had regular conferences with teachers, and teachers gave support through "awards" and "praise" (65).

4. One to two periods per week were devoted to extensive reading.

Note that this is a version of "extensive reading" (free reading with some accountability), and has a few features that may not be optimal: book access was limited, incentives were used (for evidence showing the lack of positive effect of incentives, see McQuillan 1997), and reading was massed (all at once), rather than distributed (some reading each day; see Pilgreen 2000 for suggestive evidence that distributed SSR is a better option).

The readers responded to a questionnaire after two years, the comparisons after one year. Readers reported reading more, reporting that they typically read about two hours per week, compared to about a half-hour per week for comparisons. Those in the extensive reading group also reported reading an average of twenty-six books over the last year, while comparisons only reported reading five. There was, however, considerable variation within the reader group, with some reading over a hundred books in the last year, others very few. Those in the extensive reading group reported a modest increase in interest in reading, with 7 percent reporting that their interest in reading increased "a great deal" and 62 percent reporting that it had increased "moderately." Only 4 percent reported a decline in interest in reading. Readers also reported increased confidence in reading English. For example, 74 percent agreed with the statement "I can read English books independently without much help from the teacher," as compared to 68 percent of the comparisons.

Readers also felt that they had improved; most felt that reading had improved their vocabulary (77 percent), with less perceived improvement with other aspects of language competence (62 percent felt reading improved their reading comprehension, 50 percent that it had improved their writing, 46 percent their grammar, and 19 percent their speaking).

This extensive reading program was clearly successful—there was a clear increase in reading, a modest increase in interest in reading (with clearly few negative reactions), and perceived improvement . With more access, less acountability, and distributed reading times, it might have done even better.

Subjects in Yang (2001) were students in four evening adult EFL classes in Hong Kong. All had passed an exam at a level equal to 450 on the TOEFL in grade 11. They attended class for three (consecutive) hours per week for a total of fifteen weeks. Students in two classes (A and B below) read two Agatha Christie novels in addition to the reading materials done by all students in all four classes. Students read about forty pages per week. About an hour was spent in class per week discussing the books (" . . . plots, characters, and social issues students found in the book and how those issues could be related to present day life" [455]).

The pre- and posttests were identical, a multiple choice test of "grammar, sentence structure and usage" (454–5). Yang performed an omnibus Analysis of Variance (ANOVA), which revealed "strong evidence that at least one class is different from the rest" (457) but did not perform post-hoc comparisons. He noted, however, that classes A and B made about twice the gains that the other two classes made. Combing scores for classes A and B (the readers), and C and D (nonreaders), I calculated an effect size of 6.3, which is enormous and easily statistically significant (posttest means for readers $= 74.6$, standard deviation $(sd) = 1.26$; posttest means for nonreaders $= 66.9$, standard deviation $= 1.18$; pretest scores were nearly identical for all four groups).

Results of a questionnaire administered showed that most readers understood the books, and felt that reading was beneficial. Only 20 percent had read a novel in English before. As Yang points out, there are confounds. Those who did the reading spent more time on English, and also had writing assignments related to the novels. His conclusion is reasonable: " . . . the extra time on reading in English is time well spent" (460).

Of course, one could argue that extra time spent doing grammar is also well spent, but studies of in-class sustained silent reading and related programs in which students spend the same time in skill-building and reading show reading to be more effective, as noted in the text. Also as noted in the text, Lao and Krashen (2000) reported that university EFL students in Hong Kong who participated in a popular literature-based class made greater gains in vocabulary and reading rate than students in traditional classes. Students in the literature class reported more reading outside of school, but those in the comparison class spent more time watching TV and movies in English, used English more in conversation, and spent significantly more time in academic study of English. These results confirm that time spent in reading is indeed very well spent.

2. Horst, Cobb, and Meara (1998) provide evidence supporting the hypothesis that vocabulary is acquired via reading, but conclude that reading is "not a very effective way" for those at lower levels of competence to increase their vocabulary. Subjects in their study were "low-intermediate" students of English as a foreign language in Oman. Students read a simplified version of *The Mayor of Casterbridge*, consisting of 21,232 words. The procedure was "rather unorthodox": students followed along in the text while the story was read aloud in class by the teacher in six class sessions. This was done to ensure subjects covered the entire text and to prevent students from looking up words while reading. Horst, Cobb, and Meara assure us that students were "absorbed by the story" (211).

Horst, Cobb, and Meara constructed a multiple-choice vocabulary test of 45 words considered to be potentially unknown to the subjects. On a pretest given a week before the reading, subjects averaged 21.64 correct ($sd = 6.45$). Thus, 23 words remained for potential acquisition. On the posttest following the reading, subjects averaged 26.26 correct ($sd = 6.43$), a gain of 4.62, or 22 percent (effect size based on pre- and posttests = 0.72). This rate is somewhat higher than that seen in previous studies using adult second language acquirers (e.g., Pitts, White, and Krashen 1989; Day, Omura, and Hiramatsu 1991; Dupuy and Krashen 1993), which Horst, Cobb, and Meara attribute to the fact that a longer text was used. They describe the increase as "small but substantial" (214). Despite this conclusion, Horst, Cobb, and Meara argue that for acquirers at this level, reading is not enough. Reading a 20,000-word book resulted in a 5-word increase: Even if they read one such book a week, this would translate into a gain of only 250 words per year, insufficient progress to reach the 5,000-word level considered by some to be the minimum to read authentic texts. Since students have "limited time," "vocabulary growth needs to proceed more rapidly" (221).

There are several problems with this conclusion:

1. It is not clear that direct teaching results in true acquisition of vocabulary; direct teaching results in learning, not acquisition, a fragile kind of knowledge that is unavailable unless stringent conditions are met, and that fades fairly quickly with time (see Chapters 1 and 4).

2. The treatment may have underestimated the impact of reading. As noted above, the students did not read at their own pace, but followed along in the text as it was read aloud, a method that prevents the rereading and pausing that naturally occur with reading. In addition, subjects may have acquired words from the text not included in the test. (And, of course, readers get other linguistic benefits from reading, such as better grammatical development and acquisition of "planned discourse," as well as knowledge and pleasure; see text.)

3. There is no evidence that those who have reached the 5,000-word level did it via direct instruction and study of vocabulary. Native speakers with good vocabularies, in fact, attribute their attainments to reading, not study. Smith and Supanich (1984) tested 456 company presidents and reported that they had significantly larger vocabulary scores than a comparison group of adults did. When asked if they had made an effort to increase their vocabulary since leaving school, 54.5 percent said they had. When asked what they did to increase their vocabulary, about half of the 54.5 percent mentioned reading. Only 14 percent of those who tried to increase their vocabulary (3 percent of the total group) mentioned the use of vocabulary books. Smith and Supanich's presidents were more advanced than the subjects in Horst, Cobb, and Meara; it would be of great interest, however, to determine how second-language and foreign-language acquirers who are successful in reaching the 5,000-word goal did it. It is hard to imagine that they studied 5,000 flash cards.

3

Current Issues and Controversies: Does Grammar Teaching Work? What About "Comprehensible Output"?

I n this chapter, I examine two current issues in second-language research and teaching, beginning with what is certainly the most persistent question in the field: the role of grammar. I then examine a recent claim, that we acquire language by "comprehensible output."

The Role of Grammar

In Krashen (1992, 1993a) I argued that studies that attempted to demonstrate the efficacy of direct instruction in grammar showed only that grammar teaching has a peripheral effect. I review here a number of studies that have appeared since that time, and come to the same conclusion, in disagreement with the researchers themselves, who in nearly every case conclude that they have shown that grammar instruction and focusing on form works.

I define direct grammar instruction here as consisting of two components: (1) focus on form and (2) presentation of the rule. It is possible to do (1) without (2), that is, focus students on form without presenting a rule. This is done in several studies described below. It is not, however, possible to do (2) without (1): when we present a rule, we are also focusing students on form.

Condition (2) can take one of two forms. In one version, the students are given the rule: this has been termed *deductive* grammar learning. In another version, the students are asked to try to figure out the rule on their own (*inductive* rule learning). The latter version is termed *rule search* in some of the studies discussed here. It is not acquisition because the goal is the discovery of an explicit rule.

I first review a set of experiments in which the impact of direct instruction in grammar is measured directly. I then review studies in which it is claimed that the impact of grammar can be felt not only on grammar tests but on "free-response" tests as well.

30

Experimental Studies Claiming to Show an Effect for Grammar

The studies reviewed in this section have several characteristics in common:

1. Subjects were experienced adult language students, which means they were used to direct teaching of grammar, expected it, and had survived it.

2. Comparison groups had either no treatment at all, or received what can only be described as impoverished comprehensible input. Comparison subjects, we are told, were sometimes focused on meaning, but this focus was always in an extremely contrived situation in which context and interest was minimal. In addition, it is clear from some of the studies that some of the comparison students were, in fact, focused on form. These studies, thus, investigated only the impact of more direct instruction (more focus on form and more explicit presentation of rules) versus less, not learning versus acquisition—contrary to what some of the investigators claim.

3. Tests were given soon after the treatment was finished; thus, only the short-term effect of conscious learning was investigated.

4. In the studies discussed in this section, the three conditions for Monitor use (see Chapter 1) were met on all measures used. (I reserve for the second section studies in which the measures are claimed to be "free-response" or Monitor-free.) I repeat here the conditions for Monitor use:
   1. The acquirer must know the rule. In the studies reviewed here, subjects had thoroughly studied the rules that were being tested.
   2. The acquirer must be thinking about correctness, or focused on form. This was clearly the case for all experimental groups discussed here, and was often the case for the comparison group as well.
   3. The acquirer must have time. In all measures used in the studies reviewed here, subjects had time to apply the rules they had studied. While it is claimed that the "time" condition was not satisfied in several of the studies, in only one case was time pressure quantified, and I argue that these results show that there was sufficient time for rules to be applied.

The consistent result is that those who had more rule-based instruction and form-focus did better, but in nearly all cases the effect is quite modest and some cases it is completely absent. The studies thus only show that more instruction means a bit more consciously learned competence, a conclusion that is consistent with the claims of the Monitor hypothesis (Krashen 1982).

Master (1994)

Subjects: Subjects were university ESL students at UCLA and California State University, Fresno. All were considered to be at the intermediate level and most (72 percent in the UCLA sample, 69 percent in the Fresno sample) had studied the target rule, the English article, before the treatment occurred.

Table 3–1
Improvement on a Test of Article Use

STUDY 1: UCLA	PRETEST	POSTTEST	GAIN
Experimental	26.8	29.1	6.50%
Control	26.6	27.2	2%
STUDY 2: FRESNO	PRETEST	POSTTEST	GAIN
Experimental	23.8	26.9	9%
Control	19.7	20.8	1%

(*Source*: Master 1994)

Treatment: Experimental subjects received six hours of systematic direct instruction on the article over a nine-week period.

Comparison group: Subjects in comparison groups had instruction on writing during the experimental period. Errors in articles were corrected on essays, but there was no formal teaching of the article in these classes during this time.

Measure: The same measure was used as a pre- and posttest, a fill-in-the-blanks test in which students supplied the correct form of the article. Master provides these examples, some involving just one sentence: *Carlos is____student at our university;* some involving pairs of sentences: *Once there were many trees here. Now,____trees are gone;* and others involving a paragraph:

> *____favorite food of____jaguar is____wild pig.____wild pigs move in____bands of fifteen to twenty. They have____great courage and____strength in____groups.*

This measure clearly focuses students on form. Master suggests, however, that the test measured acquisition, because "subjects were given the test without prior announcement and they were only given enough time to answer without deliberating upon their responses. It was hoped that the test would thus reflect spontaneous knowledge" (232). The nature of the time constraint was not discussed in any more detail.

Results: Table 3–1 provides the results of the original study (UCLA) and a replication (Fresno). Master reports that experimental group gains were statistically significant, but comparison group gains came close, reaching the one-tail .10 level in the UCLA study and falling just short of this level in the Fresno study.

Most important, the gains were very modest: After six hours of intensive study, the two experimental groups gained only 6.5 percent and 9 percent, respectively. Master also calculated the effect size for the difference in gain scores between the experimental and control groups in the UCLA study, based on the means and standard deviations (*sd*), and reported an effect size (*d*) of .664.

Rather than demonstrating that instruction works, Master has confirmed the limits of conscious learning: using subjects who are supportive of and experienced with grammar learning (international students at the university level), and who underwent intensive study (actually review in most cases) of the target rules, and using a discrete-point grammar test focused exclusively on the target rule administered very soon after the treatment, gains were very modest. The average UCLA student went from about a C grade to a low B, while Fresno students went from about a C− or D+ to a C.

Master also reported no significant correlation between amount of formal study and performance on the pretest, confirming the inefficacy of instruction. He also reported no significant correlation between length of residence in the United States and article pretest performance. It would be interesting to see if amount of pleasure reading and article use are related, as other studies have reported a clear relationship between acquisition of complex syntactic forms and reading (Lee, Krashen, and Gribbons 1996; Stokes, Krashen, and Kartchner 1998).

Leeman, Aregagoitia, Fridman, and Doughty (1995)

Subjects: Subjects were sixth-semester university-level students of Spanish as a foreign language.

Treatment: Leeman et al. examined the impact of focusing on form without explicit rule teaching. Subjects in a focus-on-form condition read passages with target verb forms (preterit and imperfect) underlined and highlighted, with different colors for different forms, while paying special attention to verb forms and their meanings. Students then answered questions based on the passage while paying attention to form, then discussed the readings and questions in class, paying attention to the formal aspects of their output and to the teacher's corrections, then participated in a debate while focusing on correctness of verb forms, and finally viewed the debate on video and evaluated their classmates' performance. All students had studied these verb forms previously.

Comparison group: Comparison students did similar activities without a focus on form.

Measures: Subjects wrote an essay one week before the treatment and five weeks afterward, a cloze test that focused them on the target items, given three days before and three days after the treatment, and participated in a debate two weeks before and one week after the treatment. This debate was similar to the debate included in the treatment (231–32).

Results: There was no difference in gains between pre- and posttests for the essay and cloze test: Neither group showed significant gains (Table 3–2). The focus-on-form group showed a significant gain for accuracy in using the target verb form in the debate.

Even the gain on the debate, however, does not demonstrate acquisition. First, only five subjects did both the pre- and post-debate. Three of the subjects produced hardly any verb forms with the imperfect in either debate, and three produced fewer than ten instances of the preterit on the posttest debate. Thus, Leeman et al.'s results are really based on the performance of at most three subjects. One can argue that the time constraints of the debate prevented the subjects from applying their conscious knowledge. But by the time subjects did the final (third) debate, they had done two debates before, and had discussed and read about the material. They were thus

Table 3–2
Increase in Accuracy in Use of Preterit and Imperfect in Spanish

	n	PRE	POST	d
DEBATE				
Focus on Form	5	66	85.1	1.67
Control	10	76.8	79.2	0.03
ESSAYS				
Focus on Form	10	77.9	82.5	0.24
Control	10	68.2	69.4	0.11
CLOZE				
Focus on Form	5	74	72.4	−0.25
Control	10	72	69.2	−0.49

effect sizes calculated from p-levels
(*Source*: Leeman et al. 1995)

prepared, to at least some extent. In addition, we do not know how great the time pressure was during the actual performance of the debate.

At best, this study shows only that one can increase accuracy in semiprepared oral presentations for a few college students who were survivors in Spanish (sixth semester) after a strong dose of focus on form on a rule they had already studied. In addition, the finding that there was absolutely no gain for the other two measures is strong evidence that the treatment was not effective.

Robinson (1995)

Subjects: Subjects were university students enrolled in intermediate ESL classes, which strongly suggests that they were accustomed to formal grammar learning and expected it.

Treatment: Robinson employed four conditions, but the results of only three are discussed here (in one condition, "implicit learning," subjects viewed sentences and were then tested on the position of words appearing in the sentences). In all conditions, subjects viewed twenty sentences exemplifying a "hard" rule of English (pseudo-cleft) and ten exemplifying an "easy" rule (subject-verb inversion is allowed with adverbials of location, but not adverbials of time). The three conditions of interest were these:

1. The incidental condition was considered to be acquisition. After each sentence, subjects were asked to answer a yes/no question intended to focus the subject on meaning. It must be pointed out, however, that that this is an extremely impoverished acquisition environment, with practically no context and no message

Table 3–3
Differences Among Groups of Learners

RULE TYPE	INCIDENTAL	RULE SEARCH	INSTRUCTED
Easy	73% (14.6/20)	70% (14/20)	85% (17/20)
Hard	59% (11.8/20)	56% (11.2/20)	67% (14.4/20)

(*Source*: Robinson 1995)

of interest. In addition, the experimental situation itself promoted a focus on form, as we will see below, and we have no idea whether the subjects were developmentally ready to acquire the target rules, that is, whether the rules were at $i + 1$.

2. In the rule-search condition, subjects were asked to try to figure out the rules. After each stimulus sentence, subjects were asked if they had made progress in doing so.

3. In the instructed condition, subjects read explanations of the hard and easy rules. Questions after each sentence dealt with form, e.g., "Did the subject of the sentence come before the verb?"

Each condition promoted successively greater focus on form, and provided greater knowledge of the target rule. If instruction is successful, its effects should increase with each condition, moving from 1 to 3.

Measure: The measure was a grammaticality judgment test given immediately after the treatment, with twenty sentences for each rule.

Results: Robinson does not present the raw data; my Table 3–3 was read from his Figure 1 (320). It was not possible to calculate effect sizes, because standard deviations were not provided, nor were precise p-levels reported for post-hoc comparisons.

While instructed learners were significantly better than the other groups for easy rules, they were only significantly better than rule-searchers for hard rules. Rule-searchers were not better than incidental students. As usual, the effect was modest: the instructed group got 17 right out of 20 on the easy rule, while the incidental group got 14.6 right out of 20. Also, the effect was only demonstrated to be short-term, and was only significant for the "easy" rule, the one that was more consciously learnable. Robinson reported that most subjects in all conditions were, in fact, focused on form: fifteen of the twenty-six "incidental" subjects said that they looked for rules (compared to twenty in the "instruction" and "rule-search" conditions). For all conditions, those who said they could verbalize the rule did a little better, but differences were not statistically significant. In other words, those who felt they knew the rule well did not do much better than those with a more vague understanding (Table 3–4).

Robinson thus does not show that learning is superior to acquisition. Rather, this study has little to do with acquisition and confirms only that experimental situations that focus students on form heavily and that provide explicit knowledge of the rule produce small advantages for accuracy on form-based tests in the short run. This

Table 3–4

Effect of Ability of Verbalize Rule on Performance

| | INCIDENTAL | | INSTRUCTED | |
	CAN STATE RULE	CANNOT STATE RULE	CAN STATE RULE	CANNOT STATE RULE
Easy	72%	75%	75%	85%
Hard	57%	65%	66%	70%

(*Source*: Robinson 1995)

study only confirms that we can make small improvements in processes that the brain does poorly in the first place.

Robinson (1997)

Subjects: As in the previous study, subjects were intermediate-level students of English as a second language at the university level; that is, experienced formal learners.

Treatment: The treatment was similar to the one used in the previous study. This time the target rule was dative alternation; that is, with one-syllable verbs one can say both

1. *John gave the cake to Mary,* and

2. *John gave Mary the cake*

but with verbs with more than one syllable, both versions are not possible:

3. John donated money to the church.

4. *John donated the church money.

*= Ungrammatical sentence
(Robinson notes that this is a simplified version of the actual rule.)

All subjects viewed fifty-five sentences, corresponding to sentences 1, 2, and 3 above, and nonsense words were used for verbs to control for prior knowledge. The incidental and instructed conditions were similar to those used in Robinson (1995). The third condition of interest to us here was an "enhanced" condition in which crucial aspects of the stimulus sentences were put in boxes to make them more salient: this condition thus encouraged focus on form without rule presentation.

Results: Table 3–5 presents results for novel grammatical and ungrammatical sentences on a grammaticality judgment task.

While the slight superiority for the instructed group in judging grammatical sentences is typical of what one finds in these studies, for ungrammatical sentences the advantage is much larger than usual. Similar results were found for accuracy and reaction time: The incidental and enhanced groups took about twice as long to make judgments. Again, it is reasonable to assume that little acquisition took place in any of the conditions in this study. First, dative alternation is, most likely, a late-acquired rule. Second, subjects in the incidental and enhanced conditions were given emaciated

Table 3–5
Performance for Grammaticality Judgments

	INCIDENTAL	ENHANCED	INSTRUCTED
Grammatical	87%	75%	94%
Ungrammatical	36%	46%	81%

(*Source*: Robinson 1997)

comprehensible input. Third, subjects in the incidental condition were also concerned with form: Robinson reported that about one-half of the subjects in the incidental and enhanced conditions said they tried to figure out the rule (241).

Clearly, the subjects in the instructed condition were the only ones who had extensive conscious knowledge of the target rule: no subject in the other conditions could verbalize the "critical factor" governing dative alternation (244). Compare this to Robinson (1995), in which many subjects succeeded in figuring out the rule (7/20 in the incidental and rule-search conditions); clearly dative alternation is a hard rule to induce. The small amount of acquisition and learning developed by the incidental and enhanced groups (as well as their previous knowledge) was apparently enough to confirm that sentences were grammatical, but this knowledge was not enough to make accurate judgments on ungrammatical sentences.

Once again, this study does not compare acquisition and learning. Rather, it compares the impact of different amounts of form-focus and consciously learned competence on performance on a grammaticality judgment test, given immediately after the treatment took place. The instructed group had had the most focus on form and had conscious knowledge of rule, while the others had no idea of what the rule was. It is not at all surprising that the instructed group did better when taking a test in which they had time and were focused on form.

De Graaff (1997)

Subjects: Subjects were experienced formal learners: All were university students. They were described as monolingual speakers of Dutch, but all had studied English, French, and German for four to six years in school.

Treatment: De Graaff describes the two conditions used in his study as similar to the rule-search and instructed conditions used in Robinson (1995), described above. Two groups of subjects studied four target structures in an artificial language based on Esperanto for a total of fifteen hours. The "implicit" group was similar to Robinson's rule-search group. They were focused on form but were not provided with an explanation of the rules, while the explicit group was. Both groups received "immediate feedback" on the correctness of their responses during exercises.

Measure: As in other studies of this kind, all measures focused the subjects on form. The grammaticality judgment test was, however, given under two conditions, one with time pressure ("participants were instructed to carry out the task as quickly

Table 3–6

Percentage Correct on Posttests and Delayed Posttests

	IMPLICIT		EXPLICIT	
	POSTTEST	DELAYED POSTTEST	POSTTEST	DELAYED POSTTEST
Gramm. judgment				
—no time pressure	68	68	78	75
—with time pressure	66	66	74	75
Gap-filling test	62	58	70	65

delayed posttest given five weeks after treatment
(*Source*: de Graaff 1997)

as possible" [259]). Also included was a grammar test; this was a fill-in-the-blanks test "without time pressure" (259). Dutch translations of each sentence were provided. Tests were given immediately after the treatment and also five weeks later.

Results: I present de Graaff's results in Table 3–6. Once again, the data was read from graphs.

As indicated in Table 3–6, the explicit group was better on all measures, confirming that for form-based language learning, subjects who are given more information about form do better than subjects given less information about form. Considering that the treatment lasted fifteen hours and four structures were taught, differences were modest. There was little deterioration of performance five weeks later, which is also consistent with the results of other studies: It usually takes somewhat longer for loss to occur (Krashen 1994a; see discussion below).

De Graaff also reported that subjects did slightly better on the grammaticality judgment task when they had no time pressure, but the difference was statistically significant for only one of four target structures. Fortunately, de Graaff measured reaction times in both conditions. With time pressure, subjects took an average of 7 seconds on the immediate posttest and 6.3 seconds on the delayed posttest. Without time pressure, they took 12.7 and 8.9 seconds, respectively. Thus, both time pressured and non–time pressured conditions may have allowed enough time to access the conscious Monitor, as de Graaff notes (271). The time pressure condition may not have provided as much pressure as real conversation, in which the speaker must contend with the temporal demands of having a conversational partner.

De Graaff's results are thus fully consistent with the supposition that this study involved little acquisition; it was a study of conscious learning.

Manley and Calk (1997)

Subjects: Subjects were thirteen university students enrolled in third-year French.

Treatment: Subjects participated in four different lessons, each focused on a different target rule. Rules used were those found to give students problems on an

Table 3–7

Number of Errors Committed on Compositions

TARGET RULE:	PRETREATMENT		FINAL	
	ERRORS	ERRORS/SUBJ.	ERRORS	ERRORS/SUBJ.
Passé composé	28	2.2	34	2.6
Noun/adj agreement	40	3.1	15	1.2
Possessive adjective	17	1.3	4	0.31
Definite article	17	1.3	6	0.46

(*Source*: Manley and Calk 1997)

essay done before the treatment. Manley and Calk attempted to base each lesson on a different philosophy of instruction, but the similarities far outweighed the differences: in all cases, there was an explicit presentation of the rule and practice using the rule in output activities, with a clear focus on form.

Measure: The measure was a composition written just before each lesson and a composition written at the end of the semester.

Results: Table 3–7 presents the number of errors students made on the compositions. On the basis of four separate chi square analyses, Manley and Calk conclude that grammar study helped in three out of four cases. Raters did not, however, consider the final composition to be of better overall quality than the first composition students wrote.

Once again, subjects were experienced rule learners. Nine out the thirteen felt that the grammar presented in class was useful, with four indicating it was only "somewhat" useful and none saying it was useless. In addition, subjects had been focused on form during the treatments, and knew they were being evaluated on accuracy.

A very serious flaw in this study, however, is that we do not know the length of the compositions, nor do we know how many times the target structures were attempted. Also, the presentation method used in Manley and Calk's table gives the impression that the impact of instruction was much larger than it was, because only the total number of errors was given. In Table 3–7, I also include the average number of errors per subject, which is the usual way this kind of data is reported. The impact of instruction appears very tiny when presented this way: For noun-adjective agreement, average errors per subject fell from about three to about one; for possessive adjectives, from about one to one-third; and for the definite article, from about one to about one-half. We thus see very few errors overall, and a very small effect of instruction.

Alanen (1995)

Subjects: Subjects were thirty-six adult native speakers of English, university students who had studied or were currently studying another language.

Table 3–8

Performance on Tests of Simplified Finnish

	INPUT ONLY	RULE	DIFFERENCE	*d*
Sentence completion	10.4 (32%)	20.4 (62%)	30%	1.06
Grammaticality judgment	9.6 (48%)	13.4 (67%)	19%	1.13

(*Source*: Alanen 1995)

Treatment: Subjects were given written input in a simplified version of Finnish under four conditions: input only, enhanced input, with target structures italicized, input plus explicit rules, and enhanced input plus explicit rules. The subjects had fifteen minutes to "study the materials" (270) and those who also had a rule were given an additional five minutes to study the rules.

The written input was clearly not conducive to acquisition: Subjects were presented with two short passages and sentences describing the picture, such as (English translations): "The table is on the mat," "A grapefruit and a banana are in the bowl," and "A melon is on the plate." Also, subjects were supplied with a Finnish-English glossary of all words and word forms contained in the passage.

Subjects were told to try to understand the meaning of the sentences and were also told they would be given a comprehension test after reading the passage, but given the dullness of the sentences, and the obvious pedagogical focus, it is doubtful that the subjects were swept away by the meaning. More likely, they "studied the materials," as noted above. In fact, five out of the nine input-only subjects tried to figure out the rules. There were two target rules: three suffixes indicating location, attached to the ends of nouns, and two consonant changes.

Measures: Subjects took a comprehension test in which subjects read true/false statements in English about the passage they had read, a word translation test, a sentence-completion test in which they had to complete a Finnish sentence with the correct locative suffix, and a grammaticality judgment test. All tests were given at the second (final) session.

Results: There was no difference among the groups on the comprehension test and on the word translation test. Those in the two groups that studied the rules did better on a sentence-completion test ($d = 1.06$, comparing rule without enhancement and input only). Alanen reported no significant difference for the grammaticality judgment test, but the Analysis of Variance (ANOVA) fell just short of significance ($p = .06$), and the effect size (rule versus input only) was fairly substantial ($d = 1.13$).

These results are not surprising. All conditions for Monitor use were met: the subjects in the explicit rules conditions were experienced language learners who knew the rule, or at least were presented with the rule, had time to apply it, and were focused on form. The input-only group had a very impoverished acquisition environment. This was not a comparison of acquisition versus learning.

Summary of Studies

As noted at the beginning of this chapter, all subjects in all of the studies discussed here were experienced learners: intermediate ESL students at the university level (Master 1994; Robinson 1995, 1997), intermediate or advanced foreign-language students at the university level (Leeman et al. 1995; Manley and Calk 1997), and university students with a substantial amount of experience studying foreign languages (Alanen 1995; de Graaff 1997).

In some cases, comparison groups experienced what is labeled "implicit learning," but it is not correct to describe these conditions as acquisition-rich (Alanen 1995; Robinson 1995, 1997; de Graaff 1997): only isolated sentences were presented, and subjects were quizzed on their content. There is also evidence that because of the contrived, artificial situations, many subjects in the implicit condition were focused on form, and in one study a substantial number of "implicit" subjects said that they could state the target rule (Robinson 1995).

Subjects were focused on form on all tests. Master (1994) used a fill-in-the-blanks grammar test, Alanen (1995) used a sentence-completion test that called for the target items, and Robinson (1995, 1997) and de Graaff (1997) used grammaticality judgment tests. Leeman et al. (1995) used three measures and it can be argued that there was considerable form-focus on all three: the "cloze" was actually a fill-in-the-blanks test specifically focused on the target forms, and students in the form-focus condition had recently done debate and essay activities in the treatment with a focus on getting the target items correct. Since they were also used as tests, it is reasonable to hypothesize that students knew that accuracy in the use of the target forms was the name of the game. Manley and Calk (1997) also used an essay for pre- and posttesting, but it is very likely that students realized that form was the issue.

In three instances, there was an attempt to induce some time pressure, but in the one case in which this was quantified (de Graaff 1997), it appears that there was enough time for the application of consciously learned rules.

These studies, thus, do not compare direct instruction and comprehensible input. Rather, they compare the impact of more versus less direct instruction on tests designed to measure conscious learning. Predictably, they show that more focus on form and more information presented about rules results in more conscious learning.

But not much. One can quantify the effect of conscious learning in several ways, which I have attempted to do in Table 3–9. (It was not possible to do a true meta-analysis involving effect sizes, because, as noted above, it was not possible to do the calculations for several studies.) Percentage gain of posttest over pretest may be the easiest to interpret, as it translates readily into classroom practice. As seen in Table 3–9, subjects in the studies discussed here show only a modest improvement with more direct instruction, when pre- and posttests can be compared. The only impressive gain is the debate in Leeman et al., but as noted earlier, only three subjects contributed meaningful data for this comparison.

When we estimate the effect of conscious learning by comparing the posttest performance of experimental and comparison groups, the results are similar, with only

Table 3–9
The Effect of Increasing Direct Instruction

STUDY	% GAIN	% ADV. OF EXP. GROUP
Alanen 1995: sentence completion	30%	
Alanen 1995: gram judg.	19%	
Master 1994: UCLA	6.50%	5%
Master 1994: Fresno	9%	6%
Leeman et al., 1995: debate	18.90%	
Leeman et al., 1995: essay	2.60%	
Leeman et al., 1995: cloze	−1.60%	
Robinson 1995: easy		12%
Robinson 1995: hard		8%
Robinson 1997: gram.		7%
Robinson 1997: ungram.		45%
De Graaff, 1997: gram. judg.		10%
De Graaff, 1997: gap filling		8%
Manley and Calk 1997	2% or less	

percentage gain: posttest minus pretest
percent advantage: experimental group minus comparison ("implicit") group

two of four measures used by Alanen (1995) and one condition in Robinson (1997) showing impressive results, the judgment of ungrammatical sentences. While some researchers are apparently impressed when their subjects show a 6.5 percent gain after six hours of treatment on a set of rules, few teachers would be satisfied with such results.

Thus, while investigators in all of these studies claimed that conscious learning triumphed, the data indicates that conscious learning has only a peripheral effect. Nothing has changed in the theory of language acquisition.

Consciously Learned Competence Fades

As noted earlier, in the studies discussed in this section, testing was done immediately after the treatment ended. The exception is de Graaff (1997), who also included a delayed posttest five weeks later. A delay of this length may not be long enough to see a fading of consciously learned competence. The time it takes for learned knowledge to disappear appears, however, to be a function of the intensity of training. (Manley and Calk's posttest could also be considered delayed, but we are not informed how much time there was between the treatment and the final essay. Interestingly, the structure in which accuracy decreased was the one taught first, with the longest delay between treatment and test.)

Scott and Randall (1992) reported a drop-off in accuracy on delayed tests administered only four weeks after the end of the treatment. In their study, first-year French students studied three rules, and the treatment was short: "The grammar lessons included two prereading exercises, an introductory dialogue illustrating the

Table 3–10
Impact of Grammar Study

Test	NEGATION		COMPARATIVE		REL. PRONOUNS	
	Immediate	Delayed	Immediate	Delayed	Immediate	Delayed
% correct	91	91	82	68	57	48

	NEGATION	COMPARATIVE	REL. PRONOUNS
% who improved on delayed test	36	18	0
% who got worse on delayed test	9	36	43

(*Source:* Scott and Randall 1992)

meaning of the targeted grammar structure and a one-sentence rule followed by examples in context with translations" (358). The immediate and delayed tests contained multiple-choice and completion exercises, as well as a task in which students had to write "personalized" sentences using the structure (359).

As in previous studies, subjects showed clear drops in accuracy on the delayed test. In this study, however, the decline appeared more rapid than the decline seen in other studies; this may be due to the fact that the treatment was very short, only about four minutes per rule (359)! Working much harder, however, only appears to delay the inevitable. While Day and Shapson's (1991) subjects had six weeks of instruction on the French conditional and held their gains for eleven weeks (see below for additional discussion), Harley's (1989) subjects spent eight weeks (about twelve class hours total) on the *passé composé* and *imparfait*, but they lost their advantage over a comparison group on tests administered three months later (see below for additional discussion). Subjects studied in White (1991) had five weeks of instruction on adverb placement and held their gains for five weeks, but had lost them when tested one year later. An apparent exception is Spada and Lightbown (1993), whose subjects had nine hours of instruction on English question formation over two weeks, and actually showed some improvement on a posttest administered six months after the instruction. The comparison group also improved at a comparable rate on the target structure during this time, however.[1]

Norris and Ortega (2000) claimed that there was only a slight loss in effectiveness when tests are delayed, with effect sizes dropping from 1.24 for tests given immediately after the treatment to 1.02 for delayed tests. For six studies in which two delayed tests were given, effect sizes dropped from 1.32 on the immediate tests to 1.17 on the first delayed test to 1.06 on the second. The issue, of course, is whether the delay was long enough. For the vast majority of studies reviewed by Norris and Ortega, delays of longer than three months are rare.[2]

Scholars who have studied the impact of instruction are, however, to be commended for including delayed tests in their designs. It would be helpful if this feature were also included in studies of the impact of comprehensible input and free voluntary reading in order to determine the durability of these treatments.

Summary Thus Far

This review does not include all studies in which the claim is made that grammar study is good for students. I have attempted only to discuss some current examples (see also Krashen 1993a, 1994a). Nor have I discussed the evidence supporting the alternative, comprehensible input, as this has been done in many other places (e.g., Chapter 1 of this volume; Krashen 1985, 1994a). My goal was only to illustrate that recent studies claiming to support grammar teaching over subconscious acquisition really show nothing of the sort.

The Monitor hypothesis (Krashen 1982) claims that several conditions are necessary for the successful application of consciously learned rules of grammar:

1. knowledge of the rule;
2. concern with correctness, or focus on form; and
3. sufficient time.

What is shown here is that even when we optimize the conditions for Monitor use, that is, give students plenty of instruction on a few target rules, and test them on measures in which they are focused on form and have time to apply the rules, we see little effect: The Monitor is weak (but not completely useless; see Krashen 1982). The studies reviewed here are of value, but their focus, in Smith's terms (Smith 1996), is on what the brain does not do well.

The Impact of Instruction on Free-Response Tests

In the previous section, I reviewed a number of studies that claim to show that instruction is effective. In my view, the results of these studies simply confirm that consciously learned knowledge can be displayed on a test of consciously learned knowledge, that is, on tests in which the conditions for the use of the conscious Monitor are met. I also argued that the impact of instruction is not impressive; after what is often a great deal of study and direct instruction, gains, even on grammar tests, are modest. These results only confirm that direct teaching results in a fragile kind of knowledge that is applicable only when very severe conditions are met, the conditions for Monitor use. In fact, this kind of evidence has been available to the profession informally for centuries.

The crucial test of the efficacy of instruction is whether it has an effect for Monitor-free tests given a substantial amount of time after the treatment. No study has shown that consciously learned rules have an impact on Monitor-free tests over the long term.

In this section, I review studies that, according to Appendix A in Norris and Ortega (2000), evaluated the impact of direct instruction and used "free constructed response," measures that "required participants to produce language with relatively few constraints and with meaningful communication as the goal for L2 production (e.g., oral interviews, written compositions)" (440). Of the eleven studies cited by Norris and Ortega that, it is claimed, utilized such tests, I was able to locate ten of them. None provide any evidence for the efficacy of direct instruction. One study, in fact, had nothing to do with the impact of instruction (Yang and Givon 1997) and in another it was unclear whether there was a focus on form in the treatments given to any of the groups studied (Mackey and Philip 1998). In a third, Salaberry (1997), subjects produced very few instances of the target structure on the free-response test, which made interpretation of the results difficult.

In Salaberry (1997) and in all other studies subjects had had intensive instruction on a specific target form. This was clearly not the case in studies in which it is claimed that acquisition is primarily at work; subjects in these studies were not tested after a pedagogical treatment focusing on specific rules (e.g., the morpheme studies [Bailey, Madden, and Krashen 1974]). Also, posttests were not delayed long enough for their conscious knowledge to fade; the longest delay in any of the measures in studies using free response was three months. All posttests were administered immediately after the treatment in Doughty (1991), Jourdenais, Ota, Stauffer, Boyson, and Doughty (1995), and VanPatten and Sanz (1995). Some tests were delayed in other studies, but never for more than three months (Harley 1989). The delay in White, Spada, Lightbown, and Ranta (1991) was five weeks, in Day and Shapson (1991), eleven weeks, in Salaberry (1997), one month (for the grammar test only), in Nagata (1997) and Lyster (1994), one month, and in Mackey and Philip (1998), five weeks.

Another crucial point is that comparison groups in these studies did not have exposure to the target rules in any form; they were not in an acquisition-rich environment. Thus, these studies really compare the presence and absence of formal instruction, not acquisition versus learning. Thus, regardless of the kind of test used, subjects in these studies were focused on form, in most cases were presented with the actual rule, and were tested soon after the instruction occurred. There is, however, good evidence that the conditions for the use of the conscious Monitor were met during the free-response tests.

In some cases, students took other tests that clearly had a focus on form, which confirmed for subjects that the name of the game was accurate performance on certain structures (Harley 1989; Day and Shapson 1991; Lyster 1994; White et al. 1991; VanPatten and Sanz 1995; Salaberry 1997; Nagata 1997). In several cases, subjects were actually prompted during the administration of the test to use target forms when they did not initially do so (Day and Shapson 1991; Doughty 1991; White et al. 1991) and in at least two studies (Harley 1989; Day and Shapson 1991) the test was similar in format to some class activities obviously designed to teach the target forms. In no case were subjects subjected to the time pressure that exists in regular conversation. On the oral tests, subjects were asked to describe a picture or sequence of pictures (Doughty 1991; Nagata 1997; Lyster 1994; VanPatten and Sanz 1995) or engaged in "information gap" activities in which they asked questions of a native speaker (Mackey and Philip 1998; White et al. 1991), and in two studies, tests were written (Salaberry 1997; Jourdenais et al. 1995). In Harley (1989) and Day and Shapson (1991), the oral test was an interview, but no indication is given whether time pressure existed or not. It is thus no surprise that in most cases there was a positive effect for instruction, that is, instructed groups did better than uninstructed groups even on the free-response test.

Norris and Ortega did not provide details of the studies or a description of how they arrived at their results. They also do not inform us what the effect sizes were for individual studies. I therefore review the nature of the treatment, the measure, and the results for each study available to me in which a so-called free-response measure was used. Studies are presented in the order in which they appeared in print.

Harley (1989)

Subjects: Students were English-speaking sixth graders in early total French immersion in Canada who had been receiving instruction through French since kindergarten.

Treatment: The experimental group received eight weeks of instruction on the French *passé composé* and *imparfait*, totaling about twelve hours.

Comparison group: Comparisons continued with the regular French immersion experience. There were twelve students in the experimental group and twelve in the comparison group.

Measures: The free-response measure was an oral interview "structured so that questions provided contexts for the use of the *imparfait* and the *passé composé*" (343). Students were scored on responses to three questions: "...two questions created contexts for the expression of past actions in progress, while a third question created a context for expressing habitual past action" (343). It is hard to imagine that this test could be considered as anything but a grammar test by the experimental students, a test focusing on the two target structures. Other very obvious grammar tests were given, students had just had twelve hours of instruction on these forms, and the test format was similar to some of the activities done in classes (see especially "Souvenirs do mon enfance," done in weeks 7–8, [342]).

Results: On posttests given immediately after the treatment, the experimental subjects were significantly better on the oral interview. In terms of errors in obligatory occasions, experiments moved from 42 percent on the pretest to 57 percent correct on the posttest, about 5.5 more items correct out of 36, while comparisons moved from 44 percent to 47 percent correct. I calculated an effect size of 1.20 for this improvement, based on F ratios in which pretest scores were used as covariates. On another posttest, administered three months later, both groups showed additional improvement, with experimentals improving to 63 percent and comparisons to 60 percent, with no significant difference between the groups. The comparisons, in other words, caught up, and did so without the benefit of the extra twelve hours of training.

In Table 3–11, I present raw scores as well as percentage correct. Each student was evaluated on the basis of three uses of the target structures; twelve subjects took all tests, except for the comparison post- and delayed tests.

Subjects also took two other tests. There were no differences between the groups on a composition on a topic designed to "set a past time context" (343). Compositions were scored on a five-point scale (1 = high proportion of errors, 5 = no errors). The cloze test was actually a fill-in-the-blanks grammar test, because all blanks replaced one of the two target forms; in addition, "beneath each blank was written the needed

Table 3–11
Performance on Oral Interviews, Cloze, and Composition

ORAL

	Pre %	Pre raw
Experimental	42%	15/36
Comp	44.60%	16/36
	Post %	Post raw
Experimental	57%	20.5/36
Comp	48%	14.4/30
	Delayed %	Delayed raw
Experimental	63%	23/36
Comp	60%	18/30

CLOZE

	Pre %	Pre raw
Experimental	63%	24.01
Comp	64%	24.49
	Post %	Post raw
Experimental	67%	25.5
Comp	64%	24.4
	Delayed %	Delayed raw
Experimental	68%	25.9
Comp	67%	25.4

COMPOSITION

	Pre raw
Experimental	2.85
Comp	2.92
	Post raw
Experimental	3.19
Comp	3.13
	Delayed raw
Experimental	3.34
Comp	3.06

(*Source*: Harley 1989)

verb in the *passé composé* and the *imparfait*" (343). Experimentals were better on the immediate cloze posttest but there was no significant difference on the delayed test. Inspection of raw scores and percentages indicates only very modest gains; despite twelve hours of instruction, despite both correct forms of the verbs being provided, experimentals gained only 4 percent, about 1.5 items of out 38, even on the immediate posttest.

Even with these weak results, Harley concluded that her data suggested that interventions of the kind done here "can accelerate grammatical development" (357). In my view they only confirm the weak effect of grammar teaching.

White, Spada, Lightbown, and Ranta (1991)

Treatment: Subjects were ten- to twelve-year-old French-speaking children studying English as a second language in intensive English programs, receiving five hours of English instruction per day over five months. Over a two-week period, experimental children had nine hours of direct instruction, including correction, on question-formation in English.

Comparison group: It was not possible to compare experimental group progress with that of a control group in White et al. (1991) because of administrative errors. (Spada and Lightbown [1993] used the same measure, but it was discovered that the children in the comparison group in this study also had direct instruction and correction on question-formation [213]; the teacher of the comparison group, in fact, asked more questions per hour than the experimental teachers [214]).

Measure: Subjects took an an "oral communication" task "in which students looked at sets of four pictures and asked questions until they could match one of their pictures with the picture used by the experimenter" (423). This test was considered to be "spontaneous communicative language" (424).

Results: Although no comparison with controls was possible, experimental students clearly improved. On a pretest, about 41 percent of the questions they asked on the oral test were well formed. On a posttest given immediately after the two-week instructional period, 55 percent were well formed, and on a follow-up test given five weeks later, 63 percent were well formed. Each student produced about seventeen questions per test, which meant an improvement of from about seven correct questions to about nine correct on the immediate posttest and another increase to about eleven correct on the delayed test.

In Krashen (1993a), following an exchange in Krashen (1992) and Lightbown and Pienemann (1993), I maintain that the oral communication task could have had a lot of focus of form: Students had just had nine hours of direct teaching of questions compressed into two weeks, and took other tests which clearly focused them on the formal aspects of question-formation. Moreover, according to Spada and Lightbown (1993), students were prompted when they failed to produce a *wh*-question on the test ("When students did not spontaneously produce a *wh*-question after two questions, the interviewer prompted them (e.g., Can you ask me a question with *what*?)" (Spada and Lightbown 1993, 211). In addition, the format of the oral test was quite similar to some of the pedagogical activities done during the nine hours of intensive instruction: activities included guessing games in which students "were required to ask a series of questions to discover the identity of an object/person" (Spada and Lightbown 1993, 210).

It is thus very plausible that the conditions for Monitor use were met during this test. There was focus on form, and students had studied the rule. In addition, there was no indication that there was any time pressure put on the students during the test. It was not a conversation; students apparently could take their time in asking their questions and think about the grammatical rules.

Day and Shapson (1991)

Treatment: Day and Shapson examined the impact of seventeen hours of instruction on the conditional over five to seven weeks on seventh-grade English-speaking children in a Canadian immersion program. The instruction included communicative activities but there was clear focus on form. The rules for using the conditional were explained and in some activities a student was designated to be a "monitor of French"; the student's task was to "record each time the conditional was used" in order to help students develop "conscious awareness" of their language use, "particularly with respect to the conditional" (35).

   Comparison group: The comparison group "received their normal classroom instruction" (33).

   Measure: The free-response test was an oral interview "designed to elicit the use of the conditional" (40). Students were obviously focused on form during the test: "To elicit the conditional of politeness, they (the students) were told to first ask the examiner for the microphone. If they did not use the conditional, they were asked to rephrase their request in a more polite fashion" (40). This is identical to one of the activities used in class (37) in which students were asked to rephrase sentences to make them "more polite."

   Results: Day and Shapson reported that experimental students did not make significant gains on this test, but did on two other tests that were clearly more form-focused, a grammar test and a written composition. I calculated an effect size of $d = .48$ for the oral interview (administered eleven weeks after the treatment ended), based on class means (see below). The effect size may be an underestimate, however:

1. Pretest scores for the experimental group were lower than pretest scores for the control group. The difference was not significant, however.

2. One comparison class out of six made extraordinary gains (Day and Shapson's class I). The teacher of this class reported spending five to ten hours on the conditional. Day and Shapson did not provide an analysis excluding this outlier. I did so, performing t-tests on the class means for the delayed posttest. Removing the outlier produced stronger results. The difference was not significant, but the effect size was large, $d = .92$. I then removed what appeared to be an outlier from the experimental group, class D: class D scored only 33 on the delayed posttest. Now the differences on the oral interview are clear (Table 3–12).

What is also clear, however, is that gains on the oral interview were less than on the other measures. Using all classes, including outliers, for a "cloze test" (really a fill-in-the-blanks grammar test [39]), $d = .70$, and for a written composition, scored for correct use of the conditional, $d = .71$, both larger than the effect size for the oral interview ($d = .48$). (All effect sizes were calculated for the delayed tests.) Once again, one control class, class I, was responsible for nearly all of the control group gains.

Table 3–12

Day and Shapson Results, With and Without Outliers

	MEAN OF EXP	MEAN OF CONTROLS	t	p	d
All classes included	57.8 (13.2)	51.0 (15.0)	0.837	0.42	0.48
Excluding I	57.8 (13.2)	46.4 (1.1)	1.53	0.16	0.92
Excluding I and D	62.8 (5.8)	46.4 (1.1)	2.93	0.02	2.62

Even on the grammar test, gains are disappointing after so much instruction: students improved from 19 percent correct on the pretest to 41 percent on both the posttest and delayed posttest. The grammar test had twenty-seven items, which means students improved from about five items correct to eleven. After seventeen hours of instruction, this is disappointing. It would mean about a C+ in the average classroom, and provides strong confirmation of the ineffectiveness of grammar teaching, even when all conditions for Monitor use are met.

All measures in this study, according to my interpretation, showed some impact of instruction, but all had considerable form-focus, and the tests that appear to have the most form-focus showed the biggest impact of instruction.

Doughty (1991)

Treatment: Three groups of subjects read short passages daily for ten days, presented by computer, consisting of only five to six sentences, and each sentence contained an object of preposition–type relative clause. The passages were on topics selected by the experimenter; for example, whether to disconnect the life-support system of a loved one (446). All presentations were "under computer timing control" (447). Subjects had to take comprehension tests after each session. Thus, they read short passages with awkwardly constructed sentences on topics they may or may not have really cared about, and had to try to remember what they read as they read it. This is hardly a natural situation conducive to promoting language acquisition.

Two of the three groups were focused even more on form: a Meaning-Oriented Group (MOG) received "lexical or semantic rephrasings and overall sentence-clarification . . . " (448) on the lower part of the screen. In addition, also on the lower screen, the computer highlighted and capitalized aspects of the sentence most related to relative clause formation done "in order to draw subjects' attention to the content and structure of the OBJECT OF A PREPOSITION relative clauses within the matrix sentence" (448). Subjects were not presented with a rule, but were clearly focused on form. A Rule-Oriented Group (ROG) received an "animated grammar" program that provided "instruction on relativization through a combination of explicit rule statement and on-screen sentence manipulation" (448).

Comparison group: The control group only read sentences, but, again, all sentences were relative clauses, so even this group, it can be maintained, experienced a focus on form.

Measure: The free-response test was an oral test in which subjects saw "six sets of very similar pictures depicting people involved in some sort of action" (443). Each person in the picture was labeled with a number. Subjects were asked to identify the numbered person using a phrase such as "Number 1 is the ... " The idea was to elicit the use of different kinds of relative clauses. In fact, if subjects did not use relative clauses in their responses, examiners took steps to make sure they did; for example, asking at first, "I'd like you to answer in a complete sentence," followed by more direct methods, such as providing the head noun of the relative clause, then the head noun and the relative pronoun together, and so on. The free-response test was thus clearly form-focused.

All three groups took massive pretests: subjects had to make grammaticality judgments on seventy-seven sentences containing relative clauses, do a sentence-combining task in which simple sentences were combined to form relative clauses, and take an oral test in which relative clauses were elicited. This obviously sent subjects the message that the focus of the study was the learning of the relative clause.

Results: Results for the free-response oral test were combined in Doughty's analysis with written tests (the same as the pretests, see above) that were highly form-focused. We thus have no idea if student responses on the free-response test were the same as or were different from those on grammar tests. It was not possible to estimate the true gains on the tests, as it was not clear what perfect or maximum scores were.

All groups showed gains on the combined measures of relative-clause learning, which is not a surprise, as all three were heavily focused on form and the tests encouraged more focus on form. The MOG and ROG group made equal gains, about double the gains of the control group, but it is interesting that this group did, in fact, improve. (This could be evidence for acquisition without learning, but could also be a result of inductive rule-learning, as this group was heavily focused on form because of the pretest and because of the kind of input they received.) The results of this study are thus not surprising. Two groups heavily focused on form made gains on form-based tests. A group somewhat less focused on form also made gains, but these gains were not as large. (The MOG group did far better on the daily comprehension tests, with no difference between the other two groups.)

Lyster (1994)

Treatment: In this study, eighth graders who had been in a French immersion program since age five underwent twelve hours of instruction over five weeks, on "sociolinguistic variation," the appropriate use of *tu* and *vous,* and the conditional. The treatment included "structural exercises," writing activities requiring different registers, reading, and role-plays with correction.

Comparision group: Comparison classes were also in French immersion but did not receive the treatment.

Measure: One hundred six students in five classes participated, but only twelve from each class took the free-response test, an oral test in which students were shown slides of people "in a variety of situations" and asked to respond as if they were the person: "Students were required to perform five different speech acts (such as requesting or giving directions, requesting help in math, or offering to carry books). Each speech act was produced in both an informal and formal context. Informal situations consisted of interactions with allegedly known peers, while formal situations depicted either unknown adults, the school librarian, or the math teacher" (270). All tests were given immediately after the treatment and again one month later. It is important to point out that this was not a conversation; it lacked the real time pressure that exists in conversation. Also, all students had just undergone intensive instruction on the forms demanded, and had taken a number of other form-focused tests on these forms, so it is safe to say that they were focused on form during the oral test; they knew what was expected of them.

Results: Those who underwent the training outperformed comparison students. In this test, however, Lyster only considered the *tu/vous* distinction and not the conditional: "Measures of oral production were evaluated solely in accordance with accurate and appropriate use of *tu* and *vous*" (278).

Lyster administered several other tests. On a written version of the oral production tests, experimental students were better, but this difference was due entirely to performance on *tu/vous*. In fact, "with respect to conditionals, neither experimental nor comparison classes made gains over time . . . " (278). Experimentals were also better on a written multiple-choice test. These results apparently included performance on *tu/vous* as well as the conditional, but Lyster does not say.

Lyster's study thus confirms that we can expect reasonable gains on a "structurally simple rule" (280), such as *tu/vous*, after a great deal of instruction on a test in which there is plenty of focus on form and sufficient time to access the rule: In other words, when all conditions for Monitor use are met. I should point out that this is not Lyster's conclusion. He concluded that his results support the idea that "learning may lead to acquisition" (280). I disagree. His results only confirm that a simple rule can be learned and that this knowledge can be applied when the conditions for Monitor use are met.

Mackey and Philip (1998)

Treatment: Two experimental conditions and one control condition were used. One experimental condition was a "recast" condition: it consisted of interaction with a native speaker, and each time the subject made an error in question formation, the native speaker repeated it correctly. In the "interaction only" condition, no recasts were made by the native speaker. It is difficult to claim that the recast treatment was form-focused. Getting an error recast may not promote as obvious a focus on form as more direct modes of instruction. No rule was given and no other form of direct instruction occurred. The treatment involved one session per day for one week.

Comparison group: The comparison group had no special treatment.

Measure: The free-response measure was an information-gap activity in which a subject, a nonnative speaker of English, had to ask questions of a native speaker in order to determine the differences between a picture only the nonnative speaker could see and a picture only the native speaker could see. Posttests were given immediately after the treatment, one week later, and five weeks later. No other measure was used.

Results: Mackey and Philip concluded that the recast group made better progress in question formation, that is, more subjects in this group advanced one stage or more, producing more complex and accurate versions of English questions. Before accepting this, however, it needs to be pointed out that their definition of *advancing* was simply that a subject used a more advanced form two times or more in *any* of the posttests. In addition, their entire case rests on the performance of the nine subjects in the recast group and six in the interaction group: seven out of nine of the recast subjects advanced but only one out of six of the interaction subjects advanced. Mackey and Philip report that according to a chi square analysis, this is statistically significant. It is also marginal. With such a small sample, a more appropriate statistical test is the Fisher test. According to the Fisher, the difference is still significant ($p = .04$). But this result is very fragile. If one fewer recast subject had made progress, according to the Fisher test the difference would not have been significant ($p = .12$). Mackey and Philip also dismissed the performance of the control group, merely stating, in a footnote, that the comparison of controls and recast subject was not "of interest." Two controls increased, four did not. According to the Fisher test, the difference between recast and control subjects was not statistically significant at the .05 level ($p = .08$). (In all cases above, analysis is restricted to subjects considered developmentally ready to profit from recasts.)

I am not one to regard the .05 level as an absolute standard, but the small sample size and marginal results do not inspire confidence. Even if recasted subjects did improve more than the others, it is not clear why they improved. Mackey and Philip, in fact, suggest that the recasts functioned "as part of a database for the language learner" (353). It could have served, in other words, as comprehensible input. (It should also be noted that only 26 percent of the recasts were followed by subjects' repeating or modifying their own output, suggesting that subjects tended not to regard the recasts as corrections.)

To summarize, Mackey and Philip's study does not present any clear evidence supporting formal instruction. The sample size was small, the superiority of the recast group fragile, and it is not even clear that any focus on form was involved in the treatment.

Jourdenais, Ota, Stauffer, Boyson, and Doughty (1995)

Jourdenais et al. is clearly not a study of rule acquisition or rule learning, but is a study of performance, of how much and how accurately students use a rule they have already learned in class. The target rule was the distinction between the imperfect and preterit in Spanish.

Subjects: Jourdenais et al. note that these forms "had been taught uniformly (albeit perhaps traditionally) to the participants of the study" (190). All subjects were enrolled in second-semester Spanish but "the average length of previous instruction in Spanish was 4.2 years" (192)! In other words, many or even most were false beginners with considerable previous study of Spanish, a situation that is not unusual in college foreign-language study (Loughrin-Sacco 1992; Dupuy and Krashen 1998). On a test given four weeks before the study, subjects averaged 8.14 correct out of 10 in the section requiring them to fill in blanks with either the preterit or imperfect, indicating that they had a considerable amount of conscious knowledge of this rule before the treatment.

Treatment: All subjects read a passage, a version of the Little Red Riding Hood story. One group ($n = 5$) received ordinary text, and an "enhanced" group ($n = 5$) read a text in which verbs in the preterit and imperfect were underlined and printed in a different font. The preterit verbs were, in addition, shadowed, and imperfect verbs were bolded.

Measure: Immediately after the reading was done, subjects did a writing task; this is apparently the free-response task referred to by Norris and Ortega, as no other tests were given. It is important to point out that the writing task was printed on the same sheet of paper as the sample text described just above; thus, enhanced students still had the previous experience in mind when they did the writing task; they were still focused on form. The task was to write a description of the action in a sequence of pictures that clearly called for both the preterit and imperfect. Subjects also were asked to participate in a think-aloud procedure in which they reported what they were thinking as they did the task, an activity that might have focused them even more on form. Thus, all three conditions for Monitor use were met for the enhanced subjects: subjects knew the rule, were focused on form, and had time. The nonenhanced students were less focused on form, but the other two conditions, rule knowledge and time, were met.

Results: Those in the enhanced group were more accurate in their use of the preterit and imperfect on the writing task in terms of correct forms supplied in obligatory contexts ($114/146 = 78$ percent versus $54/117 = 46$ percent; see Table 3–13), but this result was largely due to the low performance of two subjects in the nonenhanced group (ME and TD); the other three subjects in the nonenhanced group scored only slightly lower than the mean for subjects in the enhanced group. Because of the two low scorers, the effect size was very high in favor of the enhanced group ($d = 2.16$, calculated from p-values).

A crucial finding, however is that when input-only subjects attempted to use the preterit or imperfect, they got it right just as often as did enhanced subjects ($54/64 = 84$ percent compared to $114/137 = 83$ percent; see Table 3–13, a combination of several tables from Jourdenais et al.). In other words, the enhanced group's higher accuracy, their 78 percent correct in obligatory occasions, was due to the fact that they had fewer omissions. Each group was equally accurate when they tried to actually write the appropriate verb, confirming that enhancement simply reminded students to use a verb.

This study, thus, found that a focus on form through enhancement at least temporarily resulted in more use of previously learned rules in a situation that encouraged the use of conscious rules. It did not result in higher accuracy.

VanPatten and Sanz (1995)

Treatment: Subjects were third-semester university students of Spanish. The "instructed" group had two class sessions of formal instruction on direct object pronouns, that is, sentences such as "La sigue el señor" ("The man follows her") in which subjects were clearly focused on form. The treatment did not involve any production practice.

Table 3–13
Use of Previously Learned Rules of Aspect

Subject	Correct	Total ob occ[1]	Past attempts[2]
NON-ENHANCED INPUT			
ME	3	19	3
TD	3	29	5
BR	12	20	12
BF	13	18	14
ED	23	31	30
TOTAL	54	117	64
ENHANCED			
JS	21	25	23
BM	21	26	25
CA	34	42	39
JE	16	25	23`
BC	22	28	27
TOTAL	114	146	137

[1]ob occ = obligatory occasions—instances where preterit or imperfect is required
[2]past attempts = instances of attempted use of the preterit or imperfect
(*Source*: Jourdenais et al. 1995)

Comparison group: The comparison group did not receive the instruction or any special input involving the target rule.

Measure: The free-response measure was a storytelling task in which subjects had to describe a story they had just watched on video. Subjects were asked to include as much detail as possible. Subjects also took several other tests, including a test in which subjects had to describe the action in a picture by completing a sentence that clearly called for the use of direct object pronouns. Tests were given both in written and oral formats. For all oral tests, subjects sat in individual booths with headphones and microphones, and their answers were recorded.

Results: VanPatten and Sanz report that the instructed group did significantly better than the noninstructed group on all measures except for the oral narration task. This appears to conform exactly to the predictions of the Monitor hypothesis, as this task seemed to involve the least use of the conscious Monitor. The effect size (based on posttest scores) was, however, substantial ($d = .51$) and according to my calculations, the difference approached significance ($p = .07$).

It is no surprise that even the oral narrative would show some effect, that the instructed group would do somewhat better, because the conditions for Monitor use were met to some extent: Subjects had just had two concentrated hours of instruction on one rule, the test was given immediately after the treatment, and other form-based

Table 3–14
Effect Sizes from VanPatten and Sanz (1995)

	SENTENCE COMPLETION	NARRATION
Oral	1.0	0.51
Written	0.72	0.92

tests were also given. Despite the fact that the order of administration of the measures was random, a large percentage of subjects still took form-focused tests before the narrative. Also, even with an oral narrative, the time constraints of a real conversation are lacking.

Nevertheless, this test clearly invoked the Monitor less than other measures; there was obviously more focus on form in the sentence-completion test, and somewhat more time allowed in the written version of the narration test. Corresponding to this, effect sizes for all other tests were considerably larger (Table 3–14).

Nagata (1997)

Treatment: Nagata (1997) was a comparison of "rule-driven deductive feedback" versus "inductive (example-based) feedback" for first-year university students of Japanese as a foreign language. Both groups were given the rule explicitly. In response to error, the deductive group was given detailed information about the rule broken, while the inductive group was given two or three example sentences with indication of what was wrong (e.g., you used the particle "wa" but the correct particle is "o"). This study was thus not a comparison of instruction versus noninstruction or even less instruction. Both groups were heavily instructed and focused on form. (The extra example sentences scarcely qualify as comprehensible input for acquisition, as the students' focus was clearly on discovering the rule.) There was thus no comparison group with no instruction.

Measure: The free-response test was an oral test given four weeks and five days after the treatment ended. It was described as a conversation, but in the test students were asked to describe pictures, and ask questions, and Nagata notes that there were "15 target particles" in the test. There was little doubt that students were focused on form, because of the instructional treatment and the fact that they had taken other tests that clearly focused them on the target forms one week before (see below).

Results: The effect size in favor of the deductive group was substantial: $d = .96$. Once again, this study does not involve language acquisition but two versions of language learning, and there is every reason to believe students were focused on form during the free-response test. It is exactly what the title of the article says it is, "a ... comparison of deductive and inductive feedback ... "

(Note: The deductive group was also better on a fill-in-the-blanks test ($d = 1.15$) and a "sentence-completion" test ($d = .71$) administered three weeks and five days after the treatment. Nagata reported no significant difference on a translation test given immediately after the treatment and on another translation test given along with the fill-in-the-blanks and sentence-completion tests. This was clearly the case for the first translation test ($d = 0.0$) but not the second; the effect size was substantial ($d = .91$) and the t-ratio was significant at the .05 level, one-tail ($t = 1.78$).)

Yang and Givon (1997)

Yang and Givon (1997) is a comparison between pidgin-like input in an artificial language and full grammatical input using adult students for a duration of five weeks. Yang and Givon found no difference between the groups for their free-response measure ("picture description") and no raw data was provided. This study did not investigate the impact of instruction, as the methodology provided to both groups was identical.

Salaberry (1997)

Treatment: Salaberry compared "input" and "output" processing using third-semester students of Spanish at the university level. Both groups were heavily and obviously focused on form. The input group received instruction on the use of Spanish clitics similar to that provided in VanPatten and Cadierno (1993) (see also VanPatten and Sanz, 1995, discussed on page 54). The rule was explained. Students were then asked to do exercises in which they heard or read sentences. Then they were asked to select drawings that reflected the meanings of the sentences or were asked to respond to the meaning of sentence, that is, agreeing or disagreeing. They were not asked to produce the target items. There was, however, clear focus on form: the rule was explained before the exercises, and every sentence in the exercises had an example of the target rule. The output group received explanation as well, followed by more traditional activities in which they had to supply the correct form.

Comparison group: The true comparison group was a group that had no instruction at all on the target forms. The sample size was very small, with nine in the input group (only six took the follow-up test), ten in the output group, and seven in the control group.

Measure: In the free-response measure, students watched a silent video and were asked to write a "complete narration" of the story. They were given five minutes to do so. This was termed a "production" task. One might expect some impact of grammar instruction on this test, because students had just finished an intensive experience learning a specific rule and knew full well that they were taking a test, and had enough time to access the rule.

Results: Salaberry reported no difference among all three groups for performance on the free-response test, and no difference on a sentence-completion test. Neither the input nor the output condition had an impact. Subjects, however, produced very few object pronouns in doing the narrative.

Both instructed groups did better than the control group on a traditional multiple-choice grammar test, which is no surprise, as all conditions for Monitor use were met on this test. The two instructed groups did not differ from each other significantly on the grammar test, although the input group did slightly better ($d = .38$ for the immediate posttest, $d = .31$ for the follow-up test). There was little degeneration on the follow-up test, but it was given only one month after the treatment ended. (All other tests were given only immediately after the treatment.) The actual gains on the grammar test were modest, and are even less impressive when one considers that there is reason to believe the students knew at least something about clitics before the experiment began. This construction is usually introduced before the third semester. On the grammar pretest, subjects averaged 8 out of 14 correct; chance would be only 3.5 correct (there were four distractors on each item).

The results are exactly what acquisition/learning theory would predict. There was no difference at all among the groups on the free-response and sentence-completion tests despite the fact that the Monitor conditions were met to at least some extent. The instructed groups were only better than controls on a "comprehension" test, which was actually a standard discrete-point grammar test. This was the test with the most focus on form.

Summary of Studies

In this section I examine studies using free-response tests. Despite their label, students who take such tests, I conclude, are indeed focused on form, thanks to the treatment, other measures, and the nature of the tests themselves. It is thus no surprise that one sees some impact of instruction on these tests: the conditions on the use of the Monitor are met.

The Monitor hypothesis predicts that one will see more impact of instruction on tests when more conditions for the use of the Monitor are met, or when conditions are met more fully. This predicts that the free-response tests will show less impact of instruction than performance on what are clearly discrete-point grammar tests in which there is more focus on form.

Norris and Ortega reported a smaller mean effect size for studies using what they considered to be free-response measures than for studies using measures involving more focus on form (2000, 471, Table 9), which is consistent with the predictions of the Monitor hypothesis:

Selected response: choose from among alternatives = 1.46

Grammaticality judgment = .82

Constrained response (supply item in constrained environment) = 1.20

Free response = .55

Norris and Ortega's overall results are entirely consistent with the Monitor hypothesis: Measures using selected response and constrained response have the most focus on form. Grammaticality judgments focus test takers on form, but they can be done on the basis of learning or acquisition; rule knowledge is not essential. Free response typically invokes the Monitor least, but still invokes it to some extent, as argued here.

We have a clearer test of this hypothesis, however, when the same subjects take a free-response test and either a selected or a constrained-response test, the two that are the most form-focused. Of the eight studies in which free-response measures were used, I was able to find four in which the same subjects took form-focused tests as well (Table 3–15). (In Lyster 1994, the same subjects took different tests, but the free-response test was only evaluated on the basis of one target rule while the more

Table 3–15

Impact of Grammar Instruction on Different Measures in Terms of Effect Sizes

	FREE RESP.	GRAMMAR	WRITTEN
Harley	1.2	1.4	0.2
Day and Shapson	0.48	0.7	0.71
Salaberry	n.d.	0.31	
VanPatten and Sanz	0.51	1.0, 0.72	0.92

nd: no difference

form-focused tests were evaluated on the basis of two rules, making comparisons impossible.)

In Day and Shapson (1991) and VanPatten and Sanz (1995), effect sizes are clearly in the predicted direction. They seem to be in the predicted direction in Salaberry (1997) as well, but it was not possible to calculate an effect size for the narration test. In fact, because of the low incidence of target structures produced, it is not even clear that this study should be included in the analysis.

In Harley (1989), as predicted, the effect size for the oral free-response measure was less than the effect size for a grammar test. The effect size for the written test was much lower, but it is not clear that there was more focus on form on this test than on the oral test.

It is not unreasonable to suppose that a test given to students in a classroom situation preceded by intensive study of a particular grammar rule will involve some form-focus, especially when the test allows students some processing time. It should then be the case that free-response tests will produce not a zero effect but a smaller effect than traditional grammar tests. This is precisely what Norris and Ortega found. In addition, the impact of grammar study, even on grammar tests, is not spectacular. The Norris and Ortega review should not be interpreted as a triumph for direct instruction, but as fully consistent with the Monitor hypothesis. Norris and Ortega note that the vast majority (about 90 percent) of studies of the effectiveness of instruction use measures that involve "discrete and focused linguistic tasks" and that the research, consequently, has been based primarily on the application of "explicit declarative knowledge under controlled conditions, without much requirement for fluent, spontaneous use of contextualized language" (2000, 486). This was, of course, my conclusion in the first section of this chapter. Investigation of studies using free-response measures, however, shows that no matter how we label these measures, they, too, invite the use of consciously learned grammatical knowledge.

Comprehensible Output?

The comprehensible output (CO) hypothesis states that we acquire language when we attempt to transmit a message but fail and have to try again. Eventually, we arrive at the correct form of our utterance, our conversational partner finally understands, and we acquire the new form we have produced.

The originator of the comprehensible output hypothesis, Merrill Swain (Swain 1985), does not claim that CO is responsible for all or even most of our language competence. Rather, the claim is that "sometimes, under some conditions, output facilitates second language learning in ways that are different from, or enhance, those of input" (Swain and Lapkin 1995, 371). A look at the data, however, shows that even this weak claim is hard to support.

The Scarcity Argument

A problem all output hypotheses have is that output is surprisingly rare (Krashen 1994a). In the case of CO, the problem is especially severe. A recent confirmation of the scarcity of output is in Ellis, Tanaka, and Yamazaki (1994), which examined vocabulary acquisition under three conditions, tasks in which EFL students heard (1) "premodified" input (input recorded from a task performed with a native speaker and nonnative speaker who could request clarification); (2) interactionally modified input (the nonnative students could interact with the native speaker); or (3) unmodified input (input recorded from a native speaker doing the task with another native speaker). Of interest to us here is the finding that "of the 42 learners in the IM (interactionally modified) group, only seven engaged in meaning negotiation. The others simply listened" (211).

Even when acquirers do talk, they do not often make the kind of adjustments the CO hypothesis claims are useful in acquiring new forms.

- Pica (1988) concluded that instances of comprehensible output were "relatively infrequent" (45). In her study of ten one-hour interactions between low-level ESL acquirers and native speakers (teachers), only eighty-seven potential instances of comprehensible output were found, that is, interactions in which the native speaker requested "confirmation, clarification, or repetition of the NNS utterance" (93). These eighty-seven interactions contained only forty-four cases in which the nonnative speaker modified his or her output (about four per hour), and of these forty-four, only thirteen modifications involved grammatical form, about one per hour.

- In Pica, Holliday, Lewis, and Morgenthaler (1989), intermediate ESL acquirers interacted with native speakers. Because the situation in Pica (1988) did not promote negotiation (an interview), some of the conversations in this study were in situations designed to require negotiation and comprehensible output. Of 1,952 native-speaker utterances, 327 were "signals indicating clarification or confirmation of what the NNS had said" (74). In reaction to these 327 utterances, the nonnative speakers produced 116 responses containing "modified output." In other words, they produced comprehensible output in response to about 6 percent of the native speaker's utterances (116/1,952).

- Interactions were also contrived to promote negotiation in Van den Branden (1997). Eleven- and twelve-year-old speakers and acquirers of Dutch interacted with peers or with a teacher in an activity in which speakers had to describe a drawing to a partner. In peer-peer dyads, fifty-one instances of negotiation of meaning were recorded, and of these, the speaker modified their output twenty times. In peer-teacher dyads, there were forty-nine instances of negotiation of meaning and twenty instances of alteration of output. In both cases, this amounted to about one every five minutes. We do not know if the alteration improved the grammatical accuracy of the output; we are told only that "these modifications often involved, or included, formal modifications ... " (616). Even if every case resulted in improvement, however, this data confirms that even in contrived situations, comprehensible output is infrequent.

- Lyster and Ranta (1997) recorded 18.3 hours of French-immersion language arts and subject-matter lessons involving fourth and fifth graders. The lessons contained a total of 3,268 student turns, of which about one-third (1,104, or 34 percent) had at least one error. While teachers provided some kind of feedback to 62 percent of these errors, only seventy-three were in the form of a clarification request, "a feedback type that can refer to problems in either comprehensibility or accuracy, or both" (47). Of these seventy-three, twenty were followed by student repair, or correction. This amounts to about one per hour, a result very close to that reported by Pica (1988) for conversations.

- The situation in writing is similar. Cumming (1990) examined the think-aloud protocols of second-language writers, hypothesizing that instances in which writers appeared to be attending to both form and meaning at the same time are potential instances for language acquisition, according to the comprehensible output hypothesis. Only 30 percent of the verbal reports made by the writers in his sample were of this kind (490). In addition, the nature of the episodes makes it unlikely that they play a major role in language acquisition: in most of the episodes writers were searching for the right word or searching for first-language equivalents. The latter is the familiar strategy of falling back on the first language when competence is lacking in the second language (Newmark 1966).

- In Swain and Lapkin (1995), grade 8 early-French-immersion subjects were asked to write a short essay in French (one to two paragraphs) and then to edit it, and to "think aloud" as they made decisions. For the draft and editing stage combined, there were "190 occasions in which students consciously recognized a linguistic problem as a result of producing, or trying to produce, the target language" (384). This amounts to an average of 10.6 occasions per student. If students wrote a short essay every day (which they do not), this would mean about 10 chances to improve through writing per day—not very much. As was the case with Cumming's (1990) study, many of the decisions were lexical (looking for the right word), not grammatical (50 percent in the first draft). In addition, Swain and Lapkin note that there was no evidence that any of the episodes they described led to improvement.

Acquisition Without Output

There are numerous studies that confirm that we can develop extremely high levels of language and literacy competence without any language production at all (Krashen 1994a). Laboratory studies show that subjects typically acquire small but significant amounts of new vocabulary knowledge from a single exposure to an unfamiliar word in a comprehensible text (Nagy, Herman, and Anderson 1985), enough to account for expected vocabulary growth, and similar results have been reported for second-language development (Pitts, White, and Krashen 1989; Day, Omura, and Hiramatsu 1991; Dupuy and Krashen 1993). It has been argued that a similar effect exists for spelling (Krashen 1989). In addition, there are case histories of those who have developed very high levels of competence from input alone (Richard Boydell suffered from cerebral palsy and acquired language through listening and reading alone [see Krashen 1985]; Malcolm X and Richard Wright credit their literacy development to wide reading, discussed in Krashen, 1993b).

Ellis (1995) is an additional analysis of Ellis, Tanaka, and Yamazaki (1994), discussed above, and provides another instance of acquisition without output. The "premodified" group, a group that did no speaking at all, made modest but clear gains in vocabulary, gaining, in fact, more words per minute than the group that interacted with the native speaker.[3]

Does CO Lead to Language Acquisition?

Nobuyoshi and Ellis (1993) claim to have provided data showing that comprehensible output results in actual improvement. In their study, six adult EFL students in Japan of "fairly low-level proficiency" but "capable of using at least some past tense verb forms correctly" (206) were asked to participate in a jigsaw task with their teacher in which they described actions in pictures that, they were told, occurred the previous weekend or previous day. During the first session of the study, the three experimental subjects received requests for clarification if the verb was not in the past tense or if the past tense was incorrectly formed. During the second session, one week later, they received only general requests for clarification (when the teacher did not understand). The three comparison subjects received only general requests for clarification each time.

Nobuyoshi and Ellis report that comparison subjects did not improve their past tense accuracy. Two experimental subjects (E1 and E2) were able to improve their performance in response to requests for clarification at the first session, but the third experimental subject (E3) did not. Nobuyoshi and Ellis claim that E1 and E2 sustained their gains to session 2, with E1 increasing accuracy from an original level of 31 percent to 89 percent and E2 increasing from an original 45 percent to 62 percent. Nobuyoshi and Ellis conclude that their study "provides some support for the claim that 'pushing' learners to improve the accuracy of their production results not only in immediate improved performance but also in gains in accuracy over time" (208).

As Nobuyoshi and Ellis point out, however, their conclusions are based on a very small sample size. In addition, they are based on a very low number of obligatory occasions. E1, who showed the clearest gains, went from 4 correct out of 13 at session 1 to 8 correct out of 9 at session 2. E2 went from 9 correct out of 20 at session 1 to 16 correct out of 26 at session 2. E1's gains are statistically significant (Fisher Exact Test, two-tail, $p = .0115$) but E2's gains are not (chi square $= .69$). Thus, for one subject there was no evidence of the value of comprehensible output (E3), and for another, gains were not statistically significant. Data supporting a central hypothesis should be made of sterner stuff.

Note also that all three subjects had studied the past tense rule, and had been clearly focused on it in session 1. It is reasonable to expect that when subjects are focused on form, then put back in the same environment, they will be focused on form again, especially if the conversational partner is their teacher. The significant effect on E1, in other words, may have been a performance effect—E1 was simply more inclined to try to use a consciously learned rule for the past tense and was a more successful Monitor user than E2 or E3.

Van den Branden's subjects (Van den Branden 1997, discussed earlier) who participated in sessions that encouraged negotiation of meaning increased their output relative to a control group that did not engage in interaction but was not superior in grammatical accuracy. Each subject, however, had only seven to nine minutes of interaction.

Tarone and Liu (1995) suggest that CO may have played a role in the second-language development of Liu's subject, "Bob." Bob was recorded interacting with peers, with teachers, and with an "adult-friend" (Liu). Tarone and Liu note that language use was much more complex in the latter interactions, and, in general, "new structures appear first in interactions between Bob and the researcher, spread to the interactions with his peers, and appear last in his interaction with his teacher" (119). They note that it is likely that Liu provided Bob with more complex input, but also suggest that Bob's attempts to produce CO in interacting with Liu played a role. While interacting with Liu, Bob used English in a much wider range of speech acts than in the other situations, and this may have pushed Bob to "go beyond the limits of his interlanguage competence in production" (121). Tarone and Liu show that the CO hypothesis, as well as the input hypothesis, is consistent with what is known about Bob's development. As they note (123), data is lacking on the frequency of CO, which prevents us from determining whether CO resulted in language development and whether Bob produced significant quantities of CO.[4]

The Discomfort of CO

The CO hypothesis predicts that we acquire language when there is a communicative breakdown and we are "pushed to use alternative means to get across...the message...precisely, coherently, and appropriately" (Swain 1985, 248–49). In addition to the research that shows that CO is an unlikely candidate, there is additional evidence that "pushing" students to speak is unpleasant for them. When asked what aspects of foreign-language classes are the most anxiety-provoking, students put "talking" at the top of the list (Young 1990). Loughrin-Sacco (1992) reported that for students in beginning French classes, "for nearly every student...speaking was the highest anxiety-causing activity" (314).

Ten "anxious" foreign-language students interviewed by Price (1991) stated that their greatest source of anxiety "was having to speak the target language in front of their peers" (313). Of great interest here is the finding that another source of stress "was the frustration of not being able to communicate effectively" (105).

These results suggest that it is "pushed output," having to utilize structures they have not yet acquired, under demanding conditions, that students find uncomfortable. Methods based on comprehensible output put students in this situation constantly.

CO and the Interaction Hypothesis

The CO hypothesis is linked to what is sometimes called the *interaction hypothesis,* the hypothesis that we acquire language from interacting with others. As stated in this way, the interaction hypothesis is vague—is interaction necessary or just helpful? Is it the only way to acquire language or one way to acquire language? Also, what occurs during interaction that causes language acquisition?

I have argued that a part of interaction that does not contribute to language acquisition is the output produced by the language acquirer. In addition, there is evidence that a strong version of the interaction hypothesis, one that asserts that interaction is necessary for language acquisition, is not correct. Such a hypothesis denies that acquisition can occur from reading and listening. In addition to the massive data showing that reading can promote language development (e.g., Chapter 2, this volume), the results of Ellis, Tanaka, and Yamazaki (1994), discussed above, confirm that acquisition is possible without actually participating in the interaction. A weaker version of the interaction hypothesis is that interaction can be a good source of comprehensible input (Krashen 1982).

The Need Hypothesis

The CO hypothesis is closely related to the *need hypothesis.* I have never seen the need hypothesis discussed explicitly in print, but it is widely assumed to be true. The need hypothesis says that we acquire language only when we "need" to communicate, when we need to make ourselves understood. If this hypothesis is correct, language acquirers must be forced to speak the second language. The need hypothesis thus implies that submersion is a good thing, in that it forces students to try to communicate.

The need hypothesis is not correct. An excellent counterargument was presented by Garrison Keillor on the *Prairie Home Companion,* in a segment called "The Minnesota Language School." The Minnesota Language School operates on the assumption that we acquire language when we need to use it. Their method is to take someone who speaks no German at all, fly them up in a helicopter, and threaten to push them out if they don't start speaking German immediately. If the need hypothesis were correct, this would work.

According to the input hypothesis, need can be helpful when it puts the acquirer in a position to get comprehensible input. All the need in the world, however, will not result in language acquisition if there is no comprehensible input. In addition, interesting and comprehensible input will result in language acquisition whether need is present or not.

Summary and Conclusion on Comprehensible Output

The comprehensible output hypothesis has numerous difficulties:

- Output and especially comprehensible output is too scarce to make a real contribution to linguistic competence.
- High levels of linguistic competence are possible without output.
- There is no direct evidence that comprehensible output leads to language acquisition.

In addition, there is some evidence that suggests that students do not enjoy being pushed to speak.

The original impetus for the comprehensible output hypothesis was the observation that students in French immersion, despite years of input, were not as good as observers felt they should be in grammatical aspects of their second language (Swain 1985). Input, it was suggested, was therefore not enough. It can be argued, however, that we haven't yet given comprehensible input a real chance. We have yet to see how students will do if their classes are filled with comprehensible input, if they have access to a great deal of very interesting reading and listening materials (films, tapes), and if the acquisition situation is genuinely free of anxiety. (There is evidence that children in French immersion do very little pleasure reading in their second language; Romney, Romney, and Menzies (1995) reported that the French-immersion students they studied spent "an average of 3 1/2 minutes a day reading French books and one minute reading French comics, magazines and newspapers . . . " (485). By comparison, they averaged twenty-six minutes per day reading English books and seven minutes reading English language comics, magazines, and newspapers. When asked to name their favorite French author, only 3 percent of the students could name an author; in contrast, 81 percent were able to name their favorite English author.)

Given the consistent evidence for comprehensible input (Krashen 1994a) and the failure of other means of developing language competence, providing more comprehensible input seems to be a more reasonable strategy than increasing output.

Notes

1. The comparison-group teacher promoted a focus on form, frequently correcting students' use of question forms, but students in the experimental classes produced more questions and had more feedback. Spada and Lightbown point out that the comparison teacher might have emphasized form more in the months preceding the treatment, which in their view explains why this group also did well on the delayed posttest. Comparison students, however, also heard far more questions (1993, 214, Table 3). Clearly, this one study does not help us decide among competing hypotheses.

2. The discussion here is of durability of the effect. Interestingly, Norris and Ortega reported a slightly smaller effect size for studies with longer treatments, measuring treatment length in terms of hours devoted to the instruction. As they note, factors such as the complexity of the target rule and intensity of instruction were not considered in their analysis.

3. As noted earlier, only seven of the forty-two subjects in the interaction group actually spoke: Ellis, Tanaka, and Yamazaki (1994) found, however, that these seven "did not enjoy a clear advantage in either comprehension or vocabulary over those who just listened" (212).

4. Kitajima (2001) claimed that output-based activities are superior to input-based activities for learning vocabulary. In her study, five students of fifth-semester Japanese at the university level were exposed to nineteen verbs in two input-based sessions of twenty-five minutes duration each, and to twenty verbs in two sessions combining input and output (termed *output* here). Words used in the two conditions were different but were considered to be of equal difficulty. In the input sessions, students heard the target words in a meaningful context, and were then given "a simple explanation" of the word (475), which was followed by questions in which the target words were used. Students were not required to use the target word in their answers. In the output sessions, the presentation and explanation were the same as in the input session, but they were followed by activities in which students had to produce the target words in small-group discussions with other students and in class presentations. There was no difference in retention of words in a test given immediately after the presentation, but words presented in output activities were retained better on tests given one month and two months later. (No statistical tests were performed because of the small sample size.)

Does this result provide counterevidence to the input hypothesis and evidence in favor of some kind of output hypothesis? No. The input hypothesis deals with subconscious language acquisition, not conscious language learning. Very little acquisition was involved in this study. It was, rather, a comparison of the impact of different amounts of conscious practice of previously consciously learned material on retention. Consider the following points:

1. Subjects were given the definitions of the words, and were thus not required to acquire the meanings of the words from context. This study was, therefore, not a study of acquisition or new learning, but a study of retention of consciously learned vocabulary.

2. The input condition was a very weak acquisition environment: while some comprehensible input was present, students were clearly focused on form. As noted above, they were told what the target words meant and knew that they had to try to remember them. Words were initially presented in a comprehensible way, with context, but were not part of an interesting text or story. Rather, they were presented in isolated and contrived contexts. Here is an example of the kind of question used in the input condition and in the first part of the output condition.

> For example, to introduce the target word "be successful," the instructor showed a video scene of a computer room at a university and asked students questions, for example, about who became successful in the use of computers, in what fields would they be hoping to succeed, and what skills and knowledge would be required for success in those fields." (473)

> Each target word received a different scenario. It is likely that students would not be particularly fascinated by such contexts; they would not be "lost in the story" but would be fully aware that they are practicing new vocabulary words.

3. There was clear focus on form in both conditions, but students were more intensively focused on form in the output condition than in the input condition. In both conditions, subjects were aware at all times that they were learning vocabulary. In addition, subjects in the output condition were told that they would be required to actually produce the target items at the end of the session. During the output sessions, target words were available on the blackboard and students were required to use those words.

4. The conditions for Monitor use (Krashen 1982; Chapter 1, this volume) were present for all tests given. The tests clearly focused the students on form, students had been told the meanings of the words, and the tests allowed sufficient time for students to access their conscious knowledge; in no case were subjects forced to produce the words under the time constraints of ordinary conversation.

5. Subjects were all university students in their fifth semester of study of Japanese. It is thus safe to say that they were all highly successful "learners," familiar with conscious learning of language, and accustomed to it. In fact, Kitajima notes that the less diligent students in the class were not utilized in the study, those who did not attend regularly or who dropped the course while the study was taking place (475).

Kitajima's study is useful and interesting, but has little to do with language acquisition and therefore little to do with the input hypothesis. It is a study of the effect of different amounts of form-focused practice on previously learned (not acquired) vocabulary. It showed that highly trained learners remember consciously learned knowledge better when they are more intensively focused on form than when they are less intensely focused on form. It does not show that learning is better than acquisition or that output is better than input.

4

How Reading and Writing Make You Smarter, or, How Smart People Read and Write

How We Get Smart

To explain how reading and writing make you smarter, I first have to discuss how we get smart. To do this, I present a model derived largely from Graham Wallas' *The Art of Thought*, published in 1926, and Frank Smith's *Comprehension and Learning* (1975). According to this model, we go through the following stages in thinking and creating new ideas:

1. *Preparation:* In order to come up with new ideas, we have to prepare, or clarify, our current ideas and the problem we are working on. Wallas (1926) states, "our mind is not likely to give us a clear answer to any particular problem unless we set it a clear question" (44). Elbow (1973) may be referring to the same stage when he discusses "wrestling with ideas" (129) and "perception of a major mess" (131).

2. *Incubation:* In this stage, the mind goes about solving the problem. Elbow (1973, 1981) refers to this as "cooking." Incubation occurs subconsciously and automatically. When given a clearly stated problem, we involuntarily attempt to solve it.

3. *Illumination:* Illumination is the emergence of a new idea, the result of incubation. It is often perceived by the thinker as a sudden insight ("Eureka").

4. *Verification:* Ideas that emerge from the incubation stage are fragile and easily forgotten. To enter long-term memory, they need to be confirmed or verified. One conjecture is that this happens when the thinker notes that he or she has arrived at the same conclusion from a different source or when he or she discovers that someone else has the same idea.

Wallas (1926) points out that the five stages can overlap:

> ...a physiologist watching an experiment, or a business man going through his morning's letters, may, at the same time, be "incubating" on a problem which he proposed to himself a few days ago, be accumulating knowledge in "preparation"

68

for a second problem, and be "verifying" his conclusion on a third problem. Even in exploring the same problem, the mind may be unconsciously employed in preparing or verifying another aspect. (42)

A very exciting hypothesis is that the process outlined here is the gateway to long-term memory and the development of new cognitive structures. In other words, we learn by solving problems, and not by deliberate study.

Some Notes on Incubation

The incubation stage is of particular interest, because it appears to require that we do nothing when we take a break from creative work, and the mind is relaxed, not focused on the problem. Wallas (1926) noted that "in the case of the more difficult forms of creative thought . . . it is desirable that not only that there should be an interval free from conscious thought on the particular problem concerned, but also that that interval should be so spent that nothing should interfere with the free working of the unconscious processes of the mind. In those cases, the stage of incubation should include a large amount of actual relaxation" (95).

Wallas reports that he first heard of the idea of incubation from the physicist Helmholz. In a speech delivered in 1891, Helmholz described how new thoughts came to him: After previous investigation, "in all directions . . . happy ideas come unexpectedly without effort, like an inspiration . . . they have never to me when my mind was fatigued, or when I was at my working table . . . They came particularly readily during the slow ascent of wooded hills on a sunny day" (91).

Einstein clearly knew about incubation: According to Clark (1971), Einstein would "allow the subconscious to solve particularly tricky problems. 'Whenever he felt that he had come to the end of the road or into a difficult situation in his work,' his eldest son said, 'he would take refuge in music, and that would resolve all his difficulties.'" (106). Clark notes that for Einstein, "with relaxation, there would often come the solution" (106).

Csikszentmihalyi and Sawyer (1995) interviewed nine "creative" individuals, all of whom had made creative contributions in their field, were sixty or older, and were still actively involved in creative work. All mentioned that insights occurred during idle time, and several mentioned that they occurred while they were doing something else, during a "repetitive, physical activity" such as gardening, shaving, taking a walk, or taking a bath (348).

Mind On, Mind Off

This is not to say, of course, that hard work is unnecessary. Quite the opposite is true. Many studies confirm that high achievers put in a tremendous amount of work, far more than less accomplished colleagues (Simonton 1988). The hard work of thinking and problem solving comes in the preparation and verification stages, not in the incubation stage. Wallas suggests that the educated person knows how to prepare and then allow incubation to happen: the educated person "can 'put his mind on' to a chosen subject, and 'turn his mind off.'" (92). Also, the "illumination" that is the result of incubation needs to be followed by more conscious work. Ideas that arise as a result of incubation need to be evaluated (Smith 1994); our new insight may not be right.[1]

Scheduling Incubation Time and Not Being Ashamed of It

Some of Csikszentmihalyi and Sawyer's (1995) subjects actually scheduled "a period of solitary idle time that follows a period of hard work . . . many of them told us that without this solitary, quiet time, they would never have their most important ideas" (347). One respondent actually began his interview with this statement: "I'm fooling around not doing anything, which probably means this is a creative period . . . I think that people who keep themselves busy all the time are generally not creative, so I'm not ashamed of being idle" (352).

The Research on Learning by Problem Solving

There is formal and informal evidence supporting the hypothesis that we learn through solving problems. I begin with the informal evidence because, in my opinion, it is much more convincing.

The Informal Evidence

The Fox Hills Mall

It has been said that if Americans are not at home or at work, the third most likely place you will find them is in a shopping mall. I lived near the Fox Hills Mall in Culver City, California, for many years, and my experiences in this mall lend support to the hypothesis that we learn by solving problems and not by "study." After some reflection, I have come to the conclusion that I probably know about one thousand facts about the Fox Hills Mall (and I am sure you know one thousand facts about your shopping mall). I won't list them all, just enough to make the point:

1. I know where the Fox Hills mall is (corner of Slausen and Sepulveda, underneath a very short freeway).

2. I know where to park at the Fox Hills mall. There are at least twenty options for parking, and each option has its own consequences.

3. I know where the telephones are (the ones in the center of the mall are usually broken or in use; I recommend the ones in May Company), and I know where the bathrooms are.

4. I know a great deal about some of the stores in the mall, and practically nothing about the others. Of course, I know about the stores I have shopped in. I know, for example, if LensCrafters will really give you a new pair of glasses in one hour. (Actually, yes.)

How did I learn all this? Where did I get all this detailed knowledge? I never studied. The manager of the mall does not give shoppers a manual describing the mall and require them to get at least 80 percent correct on a test before they are allowed to shop. I got my knowledge of the mall the same way you learned about your mall—by finding a telephone, by buying things . . . by solving problems.

This is clearly the way all experts gain their detailed knowledge of their fields. Linus Pauling, I am sure, did not master the entire field of chemistry by studying flashcards. As Frank Smith has pointed out (Smith 1988), the "laws of learning" are irrelevant when we are involved in real problem solving. The man proposes marriage to the woman. He doesn't ask her, five minutes later, what her answer was, claiming he forgot. When the information solves a problem, when it is relevant, one repetition is often enough.

The Formal Evidence: Breaking the Intentional Learning Barrier

Experimental evidence for the hypothesis that we learn by problem solving comes from studies of "incidental learning." Hyde and Jenkins (1969) presented subjects with written words that were flashed for a brief moment, not long enough for the subjects to examine the words in detail. One group of subjects was asked to estimate the number of letters in the word (the count group). A second group was asked to determine whether the letter *e* was in the word (the *e*-search group). A third group was asked to rate the words as to their "pleasantness" (people would probably rate *tree* as more pleasant than *tire*). Hyde and Jenkins then surprised their subjects by asking them to recall as many of the words as they could. The pleasantness group remembered the most words. The pleasantness group also did just as well as a fourth group that deliberately tried to remember the words. Thus, "incidental" learning was shown to be just as effective as "intentional" learning, if the problem that the incidental learners are trying to solve is interesting enough.

Wilson and Bransford (reported in Bransford 1979) did a similar study, but added another condition, the "desert island" condition: They asked subjects to rate how important the objects denoted by the presented words (nouns) would be on a desert island. The desert island subjects remembered the words better than the group that deliberately studied.

Wilson and Branford's results are very important; they show that incidental learning can be more effective than intentional learning. In other words, they break the intentional learning barrier. In my opinion, it is very easy to break the intentional learning barrier. Many things we do in everyday life, many problems we solve (such as shopping in the Fox Hills Mall) are more interesting than the desert island condition in Wilson and Bransford's study.[2]

We now turn to the main point: how reading and writing make you smarter. To reveal the punch line early, I am going to claim that to at least some extent, "smart people" are people who have learned to read and write in ways that are consistent with the thinking process presented earlier. They use reading and writing, in other words, to solve problems. And in order to do this, they have had to overcome the lessons they learned in school.

Reading and Cognitive Development

There is little doubt that reading influences cognitive development, but it is surprisingly difficult to find direct evidence. Ravitch and Finn (1987), in their study *What Do Our 17-Year-Olds Know?* found that those seventeen-year-olds who knew more, read more: those who lived in a print-richer environment did better overall on tests of history and literature, and there was a clear relationship between the amount of reported leisure reading and performance on the literature test. Stanovich and Cunningham (1992) confirmed that college students who read more[3] did better on the same test of history and literature knowledge that Ravitch and Finn used, and this relationship held even when nonverbal ability factors were controlled.

Those who read more also do better on various measures of cultural knowledge. West and Stanovich (1991) created a cultural literacy test, a checklist of thirty names of artists, entertainers, explorers, philosophers, and scientists. Those who had more print exposure did better on this test, even when other factors, such as SAT scores (West and Stanovich 1991), age, education, exposure to television (West, Stanovich, and Mitchell 1993), and nonverbal abilities (Stanovich, West, and Harrison 1995) were controlled. Stanovich and Cunningham (1993) found that those with more print exposure did better on a test of "practical knowledge" and a test of science and social studies.[4]

Good Thinkers Read More

Studies of "good thinkers" also give us some reason to believe that reading makes you smarter. Good thinkers, however they are defined, read a great deal and have read a great deal. Simonton (1988) concluded that "omnivorous reading in childhood and adolescence correlates positively with ultimate adult success" (11). Schaefer and Anastasi (1968) reported that high school students considered to be creative read more than average students, with more creative students reporting that they read over fifty books per year. Emery and Csikszentmihalyi (1982) compared fifteen men of blue-collar background who became college professors with fifteen men of very similar background who grew up to become blue-collar workers. The future professors lived in a much more print-rich environment and did far more reading when they were young.

It thus appears to be the case that good thinkers, as a group, read more than the general population does. After a certain point, however, the relationship between the amount of reading done and thinking is less clear. Goertzel, Goertzel, and Goertzel (1978) studied three hundred "eminent personalities of our age" (subjects of biographies in the Menlo Park Library published after 1963) and reported that almost half of the group were "omnivorous readers" (11). Simonton (1984) did a reanalysis of this data, however, and found only a .12 correlation between "achieved eminence" and amount of reading done. Van Zelst and Kerr (1951) reported a modest .26 correlation between number of professional journals read regularly and productivity (published papers and inventions) in a sample of scientists (controlled for age). They also reported that the relationship between reading and productivity resulted in a bimodal curve—some less productive scientists read a great deal. Apparently, good thinkers do read a lot, but it is possible to overread. Wallas (1926) was aware of this, noting that "industrious passive reading" (48) may interfere with incubation.

Selective Reading

What may be crucial is not simply reading a lot, but reading selectively—reading what you need to read to solve the problem you are currently working on. Brazerman (1985) provides support for this idea. Brazerman examined the reading habits of top physicists, and reported that they read a great deal, visiting the library frequently to keep up with current research. They distinguished, however, between "core" and "peripheral" reading, reading carefully only what was relevant to their interests at the time.

It may be the case that reading is useful to us only when it is relevant to a problem we are working on, when it helps us gather information for preparation or verification. When we read selectively to help us solve a problem, we remember what we read. When we read material that is irrelevant, we don't remember it. This is certainly my experience. I have, it seems, nearly total recall for some articles and books I read years ago. Quite often, however, I run across an article or book on my shelf that has my underlining in it, my notes in the margin, and I have no conscious memory whatsoever of having read it, even if the book or journal is fairly recent. Whenever this happens, it is something I read because I felt I should read it, not something that related to a problem I was working on at the time.[5]

School

School tells us the opposite. School does not encourage selective reading for problem solving, but tells us that all reading is core reading, and that we should try to remember what we read. School does this by assigning a certain amount of reading for each class, and by testing us on our reading. This works against cognitive development.

Consider what happens when you have a twenty-five-page assignment to read in one evening. You read the first paragraph on the first page and, stimulated by what you read, get an idea: incubation has taken place. This is good. This is the purpose of school—new learning. Ideally, you should stop reading and write the idea down (see the section on the role of writing below). But you have twenty-four-and-a-half pages left to read! If you stop, you won't finish the assignment on time.

The problem, in other words, is that incubation and illumination occur beyond our conscious control and can happen any time. When we have rigid reading assignments, new ideas, instead of being welcomed, are an annoyance. Good thinkers need to overcome the lessons they learned in school.

Writing and Cognitive Development

Writing makes its contribution in the preparation stage. When we write, we attempt to represent our cognitive structures, our current thoughts, on the page. The act of doing this is a powerful stimulus toward creating new cognitive structures, new ideas. In terms of Wallas' model, writing prepares us for incubation.

Evidence suggests that certain writing activities such as note taking, summary writing, and answering comprehension questions help learning. According to Ladas (1980) "the preponderance of evidence strongly favors note taking" (616); students who take notes during lectures typically retain more than those who do not. Similarly,

Table 4–1
Results of Topic Knowledge Test

	CONTROL	READ ONLY	COMP Q	SUMMARY	ESSAY
Easy	4.7	7.6	7.8	6.4	7.4
Hard	4.7	3.7	9.2	6.3	11.8

(*Source*: Langer and Applebee 1987)

several studies show that students who write summaries of what they read or hear remember more than those who do not (Doctorow, Wittrock, and Marks 1978; Bretzing and Kulhavy 1979; Peper and Meyer 1986); studies also show that answering comprehension questions is more effective in promoting learning than requiring multiple-choice responses (Anderson and Biddle, cited in Langer and Applebee 1987). In these studies, however, the full benefit of writing is not tapped, because real problem solving is typically not involved.

In a series of studies, Langer and Applebee (1987) came closer to showing the impact of writing on thinking. Their third study is, in my view, the most revealing. Ninth and eleventh graders were asked to read two social studies passages, one considered easy and one considered difficult. One group simply read the passages ("read and study"), another answered comprehension questions, another wrote a summary of each passage, and another wrote an essay that required them to "reformulate and extend" the material from the passage (104). Subjects were given a variety of tests, including a "topic knowledge" test developed by Langer. The topic knowledge test was given the day after the reading and again five days later; only the results of the delayed test are discussed here.

Results for the easy passage (Table 4–1) appear to be contrary to the hypothesis that writing leads to more learning. Those who simply read the text but did not write ("read and study") did just as well as those who wrote essays, summaries, and answered comprehension questions. But the results for the harder passage were different. On the hard passage, essay writers did the best, and the read-and-study group actually did worse than those who didn't read the passage at all (control group).[6]

These results suggest that writing, especially essay writing, works best when problem solving is involved. As Langer and Applebee conclude, "if content is familiar and relationships are well-understood, writing may have no major effect at all" (131). Even the essay written in response to the hard passage does not reveal the full power of writing, however. Subjects were given only twenty minutes to write the essay, and the topic was assigned. We would get a better picture of what writing can do if we examine real writing, done by real writers, solving real problems that are important to them. The framework presented here predicts that this kind of writing results in exceptional learning, both of new concepts and facts.

Some evidence that appears to support this prediction comes from studies of scientific and artistic achievement. It is well established that good thinkers produce a great deal: "Voluminous productivity is the rule and not the exception among individuals who have made a noteworthy contribution" (Barron, cited in Simonton 1988, 60). Simonton (1988) provides some striking examples: "Darwin could claim 119 publications at the close of his career, Einstein, 248, and, in psychology Galton, 227, Binet, 277, James, 307, Freud, 330, and Maslow, 165..." (60). Simonton also reports that correlations between total productivity and citation counts range from .47 to .76 and provides additional data showing that quality and quantity are related.

Is this also evidence that writing makes you smarter? I think it is, but there are some problems with this interpretation. An obvious one is that good thinkers are typically recognized as good thinkers early in their careers, before producing much for public view. It may be the case, however, that good thinkers wrote a great deal privately before their work was known.

Another problem is the common perception that good thinkers do their best work when they are young. Simonton (1984), however, reports that quantity of work declines only slightly with age, and quality remains constant. It may be that quality actually increases with age. Simonton suggests that earlier contributions may simply get more attention:

> ...later creative offerings may not be perceived by the scientific community to be nearly as innovative as the initial milestones, yet this perception may be partly an illusion of contrast. It may be precisely because the early efforts have revolutionized the field so thoroughly that the later works, being interpreted in a new context, may seem to lack any revolutionary quality. (99)

Simonton notes that Einstein's general theory of relatively is "a contribution no less revolutionary than the special theory" produced ten years earlier. But the special theory "had changed the way scientists viewed the universe," making the general theory "look less momentous than it was" (100).

Regular Writing and New Ideas

Strong confirmation that writing helps thinking is the work of Robert Boice. In an extremely important study, Boice (1983) concluded that regularly scheduled writing sessions encouraged more writing and the emergence of more creative ideas than did "spontaneous" writing (writing when the writer "felt like it"). Boice asked college professors to write under several different conditions: not to write for several weeks (control group), to write only when they felt like it, or to write regularly at scheduled sessions each day. Subjects were asked to keep track of the number of pages written and the number of creative or novel ideas that came up. Regular daily writing resulted in about double the number of pages written and double the number of new ideas, as compared to writing when one felt like it. The control group reported the fewest number of new ideas.

This result is consistent with reports from professional writers who maintained writing schedules, regardless of mood (e.g., Wallace and Pear 1977). It is also consistent with the results of other studies by Boice (1987, 1989, 1994) showing that regular, planned writing sessions result in more writing than waiting for longer blocks of time ("binge writing"). A frequent theme in Boice's work is that inspiration does not typically precede writing in experienced writers; it is the result of writing.[7]

The Composing Process

Research in the language arts has revealed that better writers have mastered what is now known as "the composing process." These studies typically compare more advanced and successful writers with beginning and remedial writers, and have shown, among other findings, that

- Good writers engage in more planning before they start to write, but are willing to change their plans; their plans, in other words, are flexible (Emig 1971).

- Good writers are more willing to revise, and focus far more on meaning when revising. Faigley and Witte (1981) reported that advanced college writers made more content revisions and delayed mechanical and word choice changes until "they had satisfactorily dealt with their subjects" (409). Sommers (1980) has confirmed that experienced writers understand that their early drafts are tentative, and that as they go from draft to draft they come up with new ideas. Average and remedial writers don't know this, but think that all of their ideas are in their outline or first draft, and regard revision as simply making a neater version of the first draft.

The composing process works because it is in harmony with the way the brain naturally learns. Writers who use the composing process use writing for preparation by planning, and they respect the incubation process; when new ideas arise through writing they are willing (and eager) to change their plans and revise. Writers who have not mastered the composing process have a much harder time coming up with new ideas. An unwillingness to revise means an unwillingness to accept new ideas while writing. Excessive focus on mechanics and other aspects of editing while writing pulls attention away from meaning and may be a source of writer's block (Rose 1984).

Incubation and the Composing Process

One secret to coming up with good ideas through writing is, I suspect, understanding the importance of incubation. For many writers, good writing can't be rushed. Forcing writers to sit without a break and write nonstop denies the possibility of incubation: as Smith (1994) notes, "composition is not enhanced by grim determination" (131).

Blocked and fearful writers may be under the false impression that writing should always flow, and that hesitations are a sign of incompetence. Hesitations, however, are not usually true writing blocks. They may simply be signs that a problem has come up, and taking a break may help the subconscious solve the problem. This happens to me probably a hundred times a day: a problem with word choice, a discovery that I have contradicted myself, a vague malaise that the arguments are not in the right order, and so forth. At least half the time, a very short break, even two minutes or less, is enough to solve the problem. And a solved problem often means new learning, a deeper understanding. (Note: I took five breaks in writing this paragraph, during which time I filed some papers, took some vitamins, and checked my email.)

Many professionals have recognized this: Irving Stone (cited in Winokur 1990) noted that "when I have trouble writing, I step outside my studio into the garden and pull weeds until my mind clears . . . " (325). Richard Condon (cited in Murray 1990) says "I've never been blocked, but there are times when the words won't come. When I feel dried-up, I deal myself a few games of solitaire . . . " (72).

Writing and Illumination

Thus far, we have been discussing the role of writing in preparation. Wallas (1926) points out that writing is also valuable after incubation, when illumination has occurred. When a new idea first occurs to a thinker, before it is verified, it is fragile, it needs to be recorded: "in modern life, the range of observations and memory which may start a new thought-train is so vast that it is almost incredibly easy to forget some thought and never again pick up the train that led to it. The story may be true of the man who had so brilliant an idea that he went into his garden to thank God for it, found on rising to his knees that he had forgotten it, and never recalled it" (86). Smart people carry writing material with them.

School

School teaches us the opposite. School teaches us that we write to display what we already know, not to discover new ideas. In-class essays and essay exams that need to be done, start to finish, in one class period, actually penalize students for coming up with new ideas while writing, and certainly allow no time for incubation.

Recall your history class in high school. Your sit-down exam question is to give three reasons for the start of World War II. You think of three reasons and begin to write. Midway through your second reason, stimulated by your writing, incubation and illumination take place and you think of three better, more valid reasons for the start of World War II. You look at the clock, however, and see that you only have ten minutes left. You have to surpress the new ideas and finish writing out the original three reasons, or you will fail the exam completely.

This kind of thing happens in school not once, but thousands of times, and students learn that writing functions merely to show what they already know. Once again, good thinkers need to overcome the lessons they learned in school.

Oral Language

My focus here is on reading and writing, but I do not mean to discount the value of oral language for problem solving. There is good reason to believe that discussion can serve problem solving very well. In addition to verifying our ideas, we can also use discussion for preparation, as Elbow (1973) points out:

> If you are stuck writing or trying to figure something out, there is nothing better than finding one person, or more, to talk to. If they don't agree or have trouble understanding, so much the better—so long as their minds are not closed. This explains what happens to me and many others countless times; I write a paper, it's not very good; I discuss it with someone; after fifteen minutes of back-and-forth I say something in response to a question or argument of his and he says, "But why didn't you say that? That's good. That's clear." (49)

Conclusion

I have argued elsewhere (e.g., Chapter 2) that reading is the primary source of our competence in writing style and grammar, as well as vocabulary and spelling (see also Krashen 1993b). Figure 4–1 attempts to combine these hypotheses with the hypotheses presented in this chapter.

What remains to be discussed is what goes to the left of Reading and Writing in Figure 4–1: What do we do in class? Smith (1988) suggests an answer: "Enterprises." Enterprises are problems—real, not realistic, problems that students genuinely want to solve, problems that naturally entail reading, writing, and discussion. Finding the right enterprises is, in my view, a major goal of the teaching profession. Enterprises may include a chemistry class project in which students analyze the water in the community and publish the results in the local newspaper, writing a history of the

Figure 4–1
Impact of Reading and Writing

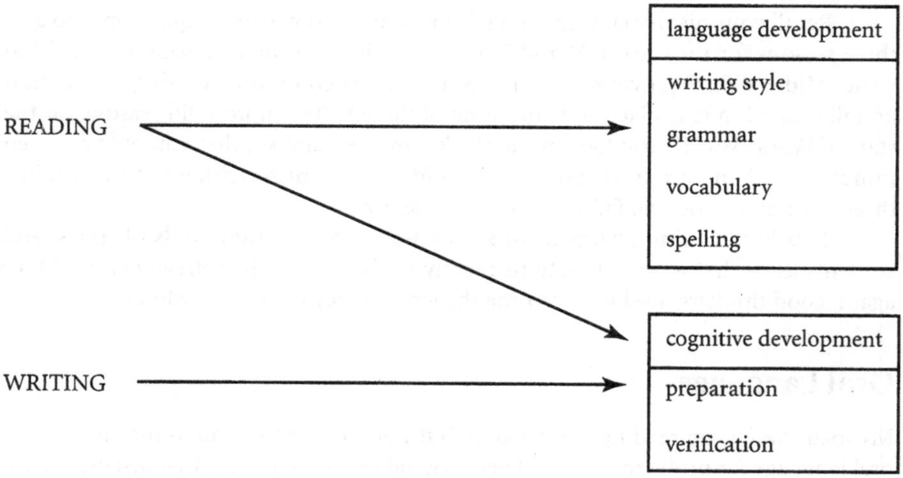

Figure 4–2
An Expanded Model

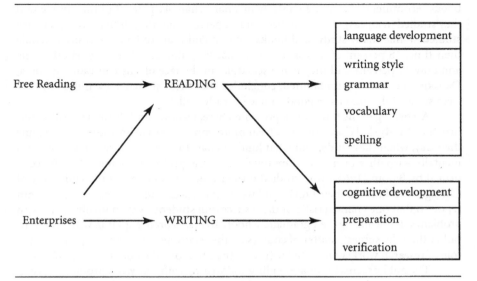

community that will become the official history and be on public record, running a small business (and keeping the profits), and writing book reviews that remain in the school library permanently for future student use, rather than writing book reports.

Figure 4–2 expands Figure 4–1, adding enterprises and free reading. An important characteristic of Figure 4–2 is that the arrows go from left to right, not from right to left. As Smith (1988) has pointed out, we have confused cause and effect in education. We do not learn parts of language and "facts" so that we can eventually read and work on real problems. We read for interest and pleasure and we engage in problem solving, real enterprises; language acquisition, literacy development, and intellectual development occur as a result.

Obstacles

If we are going to use enterprises in school, we face tremendous obstacles. The major obstacle is that many people, including professionals in education as well as the public, have a view of learning that is quite different from the one presented here. Danskin and Burnett's article, "Study Techniques of Those Superior Students," illustrates the point of view of some professionals. Danskin and Burnett (1952) analyzed the study habits of thirty-seven university students. Every student in their sample was an excellent student, ranking in the top twelve of their class.

Danskin and Burnett were quite disappointed with these students' study habits. Contrary to what is advised in study-skill courses and books, 81 percent of the students waited until the last minute to study before tests, and only 8 percent attempted to predict what questions would be on the tests. While many study-skill books recommend that students study in a hard chair, 41 percent of the sample said they studied in an easy chair or in bed, and 14 percent said they didn't care where they studied. While many study-skill books recommend that students carefully schedule their time, 48 percent of this sample said that they studied when they had the time and only 11 percent said they had a schedule. In the face of this contradictory data, Danskin and Burnett, undaunted, concluded that these students, even though they were successful, could use a good course in study skills!

According to the framework presented here, Danskin and Burnett's results confirm that "study skills" are not crucial. Far more important than how students schedule their day, when they study, and what kind of chair they sit in, is what they focus on mentally—whether or not they are involved in real problem solving. This was confirmed by Bloom (1963), who studied former graduate students at the University of Chicago who finished their Ph.D.'s and went on to successful research careers. Bloom reported that one characteristic of these successful students was an involvement with problem solving during their graduate school careers, "a preoccupation with problems rather than the subject-matter of courses ... the relatively complete acceptance of the role of research worker and scholar (rather than the role of student) ... " (257–58).

The public seems to equate reading and writing with study, not problem solving. I see evidence of this all the time. I do a fair amount of reading and writing in public, on airplanes, while waiting in offices, and so forth. Occasionally a friendly person will see me working, or just see my books and notebook, and ask, "Are you studying for a test?"

Notes

1. Incubation sometimes requires a very long break: Richard Feynman noted that "You have to do six months of very hard work first and get all the components bumping around in your head, and then you have to be idle for a couple of weeks, and then—ping—it suddenly falls into place ... " (Csikszentmihalyi and Sawyer 1995, 350). Incubation can also occur with breaks of shorter duration. Piaget told Gruber (1995) that after he worked for a few hours, "he would go for a walk, not think about very much, and when he went back to his desk his ideas would be clearer ... " (526). And it can also happen in very short breaks, a few minutes or even moments. In my experience, extremely short breaks are all that is necessary to solve many problems and loosen many blocks. In agreement with Wallas, I have found that these breaks work best when they are devoted to something fairly mindless: washing just a few dishes, filing just a few papers, or doing some light exercise.

2. Experimental evidence also suggests that problem solving is more potent for learning than additional effort or hard work (Walsh and Jenkins, 1973), than additional time on task (Craik and Tulving 1975), than additional exposures, or than repetitions of a stimulus (Bobrow and Bower 1969), and is more potent than increasing rewards (Craik and Tulving 1975).

3. Stanovich and colleagues used interesting measures of print exposure, the author recognition test and the magazine recognition test, which consist simply of checklists of authors and magazine titles. Many studies have confirmed that these simple measures are an excellent means of estimating print exposure. For a detailed discussion, see Chapter 2 of this volume.

4. Stanovich and Cunningham (1993) is an especially interesting study. Subjects were 268 North American undergraduates who filled out questionnaires related to print exposure (author, magazine, and print recognition tests) and TV exposure and who completed several tests of general knowledge. General knowledge tests included a test of practical knowledge (e.g., "What does the carburetor in an automobile do?"), a test of knowledge of science and social studies, an acronym test (items included NATO, EEC, and UHF), and checklists of names of well-known individuals in a variety of fields.

Performance on the print composite correlated highly with performance on the composite of tests of general knowledge ($r = .85$), but exposure to TV did not ($r = -.05$). Moreover, the relationship between print exposure and general knowledge held even when controlled for measures of "general cognitive ability" (nonverbal cognitive ability [Raven Matrices], reading comprehension, grade point average and TV exposure.)

Stanovich and Cunningham also compared the performance of those who scored high on a test of reading comprehension but read little, and those who scored lower on a test of reading comprehension but read more. The latter group did better on the test of general knowledge, indicating that amount of reading counts more than reading ability in terms of gaining information.

An analysis of performance on certain items of the practical knowledge test was particularly revealing. Among the questions asked was "At the time of the Normandy invasion (1944), what country was Germany's primary ally?" Those who were readers scored higher than those who were not, and TV watching made no difference. In fact, among the "low print/high TV" group, 28 percent thought that the Soviet Union was Germany's primary ally at that time. Below I also present results for the question, "Name a country in which Latin is currently the primary language." The investigators scored this liberally, accepting "Rome," "the Vatican," and "none." Once again, readers did best and TV had no impact. The overall scores of these college students are distressing, however.

	HIGH PRINT: LOW TV	HIGH PRINT: HIGH TV	LOW PRINT: LOW TV	LOW PRINT: HIGH TV
Primary Ally	33%	21%	10%	13%
Latin	48%	34%	13%	10%

5. Glueck and Jauch (1975) provide evidence that suggests that thinkers read primarily for verification and not for preparation. They found that productive scientists did get some ideas from professional journals, but relied more on their own ideas and previous work as input for their thinking.

6. Results of think-aloud protocol analysis done with eight subjects revealed that those who answered comprehension questions simply "searched the passage for the correct response, copied it . . . and never rethought that response or returned to it to change an answer . . . " (221). Summary writers searched for more relationships than did those who answered comprehension questions, but tended to maintain the temporal order of the text in their summary. Essay writers, however, used the text "to corroborate rather than find the ideas they wanted to write about" (121), thus using writing for the verification stage of Wallas' model.

7. Boice also included a fourth condition: Writers agreed to produce three pages per session, and a strong motivator was instituted: If subjects did not meet the goal on any day,

they would have to donate $15 to a "despised organization." This group wrote the most, and produced the most ideas, but was the least efficient, according to my analysis (Krashen, 2002): they produced the fewest ideas per page, and only barely made their quota, averaging just over three pages per day. Writing in all other conditions resulted in about three-fourths of an idea per page, but those in the "forced writing" condition produced about half that. It is possible that this group found writing to be aversive; they wrote just enough to avoid punishment. It would be interesting to see how much writers in such a condition continue to write after the negative consequences are removed, and to see whether the quality of their ideas was similar to those produced by the other groups.

Conclusion

In the first three chapters of this volume, I reviewed studies dealing with the effect of comprehensible input-based methodology (Chapter 1), the effect of free voluntary reading (Chapter 2), and the effect of grammar study (Chapter 3). Table 5–1 summarizes the results of studies.

The data we have so far are reasonably consistent with these generalizations. When we compare comprehensible input-based methods with traditional, form-based methods, and tests are communicative, students in comprehensible input classes clearly do better. This is supported by Asher's studies (1972, 1977) and by Isik (2000), reviewed in Chapter 1. When the test is a grammar test, there is no difference, or comprehensible input students do somewhat better. This is supported by Hammond (1988) and Winitz (1996). Students in Nikolov and Krashen (1997) who had comprehensible input, however, did only slightly better than the traditional students, but Isik's students did far better on all types of tests.

The generalization proposed here parallels results in beginning literacy development in English as a first language. I argued in Krashen (1999a) that students in whole language classes, when compared to those in classes emphasizing skill-building, did better on tests of reading comprehension, and just as well on tests of "skills" (reading nonsense words.)

Intermediate-level students in free-reading programs appear to outperform comparisons on all kinds of tests. Elley's studies allow us to compare the impact of free reading on different tests. In Elley and Mangubhai (1983), the impact of sustained silent reading tended to be larger on tests of reading comprehension than on tests of "English structures" (see Elley 1991, 387, Table 2), but in Elley (1991, 395, Table 3) the effects were similar.

Students who undergo intensive direct grammar instruction on a limited set of rules outperform those with little or no grammar instruction on tests of grammar, but the effect is modest. The Monitor hypothesis predicts no impact of grammar instruction on communicative tests, tests in which the conditions for Monitor use are not met. I have concluded that we still lack data for these kinds of tests, as students taking the "communicative" tests used in published studies were, in fact, focused on form and could apply their conscious knowledge of grammar when taking the tests. The impact of grammar instruction on these tests, however, appears to be less than on tests that are more obviously "grammar" tests and that encourage more focus on form.

Table 5–1

Summary of Studies

	GRAMMAR TEST	COMMUNICATIVE TEST
Method comparisons	CI slightly better	CI much better
FVR vs. skill-building	FVR better	FVR better
Grammar instruction	Modest impact	No data

CI = comprehensible input-based methods
FVR = free voluntary reading

I have devoted a great deal of space in this volume to criticizing studies interpreted as supporting grammar study and a relatively small percentage of space to studies supporting the comprehension hypothesis. One reason for this is that I have devoted so much space in previous publications to the latter. But another reason is because the profession has spent so much energy trying to show that grammar study works. I have presented only some of their efforts here; there are many more, but they suffer from the same flaws as those discussed here. The profession has, in my view, backed the wrong horse; to paraphrase Frank Smith, it has spent a great deal of energy studying things that the brain does not do very well.

The energy devoted to futile attempts to show that grammar study is effective has diverted energy from a more worthwhile endeavor, trying to determine the true potential of comprehensible input. In my view, the studies supporting comprehensible input, as impressive as they are, underestimate its power; there have been few attempts to really see what comprehensible input can do. What would happen if we fully utilize comprehensible input, if we use methods such as TPR, Natural Approach, and sheltered subject matter teaching, and supplement them with a super-rich print environment that includes accessible and well-stocked libraries filled with compelling books, magazines, newspapers, comic books, audiotapes, and videotapes? If we do this, my prediction is that we will see unprecedented success in our classes. We will see students who have genuinely reached the level where they can read authentic texts and can comfortably communicate with speakers of the language, students who are in a position to improve on their own.

Chapter 4 argues that we have also backed the wrong horse in other areas of education: we have backed the hypothesis that cognitive development is the result of deliberate study, instead of the hypothesis that it is the result of problem solving. I discussed some of the implications of this for reading and writing, arguing that effective uses of reading and writing aid the problem-solving process. These uses, however, are very different from and often conflict with what we learn in school.

We have thus confused cause and effect for both language acquisition and cognitive development. According to the comprehension hypothesis (aka the input hypothesis), our ability to spell, our vocabulary, our grammatical competence, and so on, are the result of comprehensible input. According to the problem-solving hypothesis, our knowledge of concepts and facts are a result of problem solving.

School makes the opposite assumption: We first learn vocabulary, learn to spell, learn grammar, and so forth, and practice in contrived situations to "automatize" them. Only after these "basics" are mastered are we allowed to actually use language for real communication. Similarly, school has assumed that only after facts and concepts are mastered are we allowed to engage in real problem solving, in real enterprises. As Frank Smith has noted, traditional schemes of education "represent the world turned upside down" (Smith 1986, 75).

Clearly, tests are a major force in promoting activities that go in the wrong direction. When a language test focuses students on form, the effect is for teachers to teach form directly. If, for example, the final test focuses on vocabulary, instruction will emphasize vocabulary lists. We know, however, that it is much more efficient to pick up vocabulary through reading (Nagy, Herman, and Anderson 1985). In other words, those who do things in the right direction do well on tests, even on those tests that focus on form, a conclusion supported by the research reviewed in Chapters 1 and 2. (Exceptions are language tests that focus on late-acquired items that even fairly advanced language students will typically not acquire without extensive reading and/or residence in the country.)

The public has assumed that some things must first be "learned," that a lot of hard work is necessary before students can go on to more interesting activities. But when students engage in real problem solving and are exposed to interesting and comprehensible input, they acquire language and learn concepts and facts much more easily. There is no need to wait. There is no need for delayed gratification.

Alfie Kohn has recognized this: "For all our talk about motivation, I think we often fail to recognize a truth that is staring us in the face: If educators are able to create the conditions under which children can become engaged with academic tasks, the acquisition of intellectual skills will probably follow" (Kohn 1993, 146).

References

Alanen, R. 1995. "Input Enhancement and Rule Presentation in Second Language Acquisition." In *Attention and Awareness in Foreign Language Learning*, edited by R. Schmidt, 259–302. Honolulu, HI: University of Hawaii, Second Language Teaching and Curriculum Center.

Alderson, J. C., C. Clapham, and D. Steel. 1997. "Metalinguistic Knowledge, Language Aptitude and Language Proficiency." *Language Teaching Research* 1:93–121.

Allen, L., J. Cipielewski, and K. Stanovich. 1992. "Multiple Indicators of Children's Reading Habits and Attitudes: Construct Validity and Cognitive Correlates." *Journal of Educational Psychology* 84:489–503.

Asher, J. 1966. "The Learning Strategy of the Total Physical Response: A Review." *The Modern Language Journal* 50 (2):79–84.

———. 1969. "The Total Physical Response Approach to the Second Language Learning." *The Modern Language Journal* 53 (1):3–17.

———. 1972. "Children's First Language as a Model for Second Language Learning." *Modern Language Journal* 56:133–39.

———. 1977. "Children Learning Another Language: A Developmental Hypothesis." *Child Development,* 58 (1–2):24–32.

Asher, J., J. Kusudo, and R. de la Torre. 1974. "Learning a Second Language Through Commands: The Second Field Test." *Modern Language Journal* 58:24–32.

Asher, J., and B. Price. 1967. "The Learning Strategy of Total Physical Response: Some Age Differences." *Child Development* 38:1219–27.

Bailey, N., C. Madden, and S. Krashen. 1974. "Is There a 'Natural Sequence' in Adult Second Language Learning?" *Language Learning* 24:235–43.

Baretta, A. 1986. "Program-Fair Language Teaching Evaluation." *TESOL Quarterly* 20:431–44.

Biber, D. 1988. *Variation Across Speech and Writing.* Cambridge: Cambridge University Press.

Bloom, B. 1963. "Report on Creativity Research by the Examiner's Office of the University of Chicago." In *Scientific Creativity,* edited by C. Taylor and F. Barron, 261–64. New York: Wiley.

Bobrow, S., and G. Bower. 1969. "Comprehension and Recall of Sentences." *Journal of Experimental Psychology* 80 (3):455–61.

Boice, R. 1983. "Contingency Management in Writing and the Appearance of Creative Ideas: Implications for the Treatment of Writing Blocks." *Behavioral Research Therapy* 21 (5): 537–43.

———. 1987. "Is Released Time an Effective Component of Faculty Development Programs?" *Research in Higher Education,* 26 (3):311–26.

———. 1989. "Procrastination, Busyness, and Bingeing." *Behavioral Research Therapy* 27 (6):605–11.

———. 1994. *How Writers Journey to Comfort and Fluency.* Westport, CT: Praeger.

Bransford, J. 1979. *Human Cognition: Learning, Understanding and Remembering.* Belmont, CA: Wadsworth.

Brazerman, C. 1985. "Physicists Reading Physics: Schema-Laden Purposes and Purpose-Laden Schema." *Written Communication* 2:3–43.

Bretzing, B., and R. Kulhavy. 1979. "Notetaking and Depth of Processing." *Contemporary Educational Psychology* 4:145–53.

Brown, M., and A. Palmer. 1988. *The Listening Approach.* New York: Longman.

Cho, K. S., and S. Krashen. 1994. "Acquisition of Vocabulary from the Sweet Valley Kids Series: Adult ESL Acquisition." *Journal of Reading* 37:662–67.

———. 2002. "Sustained Silent Reading Experiences Among Korean Teachers of English as a Foreign Language: The Effect of a Single Exposure to Interesting, Comprehensible Reading." *Reading Improvement* 38 (4):170–74.

Cipielewski, J., and K. Stanovich. 1990. "Assessing Print Exposure and Orthographic Processing Skill in Children: A Quick Measure of Reading Experience." *Journal of Educational Psychology* 82:733–40.

Clark, R. 1971. *Einstein: The Life and Times.* New York: World.

Cohen, K. 1999. "Reluctant Eighth Grade Readers Enjoy Sustained Silent Reading." *California Reader* 33 (1):22–25.

Cohen, Y. 1997. How Reading Got Me into Trouble. Class paper, Trenton State University, summer.

Constantino, R., S-Y. Lee, K.S. Cho, and S. Krashen. 1997. "Free Voluntary Reading as a Predictor of TOEFL Scores." *Applied Language Learning* 8:111–18.

Craik, F., and E. Tulving. 1975. "Depth of Processing and the Retention of Words in Episodic Memory." *Journal of Experimental Psychology: General* 104:268–94.

Csikszentmihalyi, M. 1991. *Flow: The Psychology of Optimal Experience.* New York: Harper Perennial.

Csikszentmihalyi, M., and K. Sawyer. 1995. "Creative Insight: The Social Dimension of a Solitary Moment." In *The Nature of Insight,* edited by R. Steinberg and J. Davidson, 329–61. Cambridge, MA: MIT Press.

Cumming, A. 1990. "Metalinguistic and Ideational Thinking in Second Language Composing." *Written Communication* 7:482–511.

Cummins, J. 1981. "The Role of Primary Language Development in Promoting Success for Language Minority Students." In *Schooling and Language Minority Students: A Theoretical Framework,* edited by Office of Bilingual Education, State of California, 3–49. California State University, Los Angeles: Evaluation, Dissemination and Assessment Center.

Cunningham, A., and K. Stanovich. 1990. "Assessing Print Exposure and Orthographic Processing Skill in Children: A Quick Measure of Reading Experience." *Journal of Educational Psychology* 82:733–40.

Daly, J., and D. Wilson. 1983. "Writing Apprehension, Self-Esteem, and Personality." *Research in the Teaching of English* 17:327–41.

Danskin, D., and C. Burnett. 1952. "Study Techniques of Those Superior Students." *Personnel and Guidance Journal* 31:181–86.

Day, E., and S. Shapson. 1991. "Integrating Formal Approaches to Language Teaching in French Immersion: An Experimental Study." *Language Learning* 41:25–58.

Day, R., C. Omura, and M. Hiramatsu. 1991. "Incidental Vocabulary Learning and Reading." *Reading in a Foreign Language* 7:541–51.

De Graaff, R. 1997. "The Esperanto Experiment: Effects of Explicit Instruction on Second Language Acquisition." *Studies in Second Language Acquisition* 19:249–76.

DeKeyser, R. 1993. "The Effect of Error Correction on L2 Grammar Knowledge and Oral Proficiency." *Modern Language Journal* 77:501–14.

Doctorow, M., M. Wittrock, and C. Marks. 1978. "Generative Processes in Reading Comprehension." *Journal of Educational Psychology* 70:109–18.

Doughty, C. 1991. "Second Language Instruction Does Make a Difference: Evidence from an Empirical Study of SL Relativization." *Studies in Second Language Acquisition* 13 (4):431–69.

Dupuy, B., and S. Krashen. 1993. "Incidental Vocabulary Acquisition in French as a Foreign Language." *Applied Language Learning* 4:55–63.

————. 1998. "From Lower-Division to Upper-Division Foreign Language Classes: Obstacles to Reading the Promised Land." *ITL: Review of Applied Linguistics* 199–120:1–7.

Dupuy, B., and J. McQuillan. 1997. "Handcrafted Books: Two for the Price of One." In *Successful Strategies for Extensive Reading*, edited by G. Jacobs, D. Davis, and W. Renandya. Singapore: SEAMEO Regional Language Centre.

Dupuy, B., L. Tse, and T. Cook. 1996. "Bringing Books into the Classroom: First Steps in Turning College-Level ESL Students into Readers." *TESOL Journal,* 5 (4):10–15.

Edwards, H., M. Wesche, S. Krashen, R. Clement, and B. Kruidenier. 1985. "Second-Language Acquisition Through Subject-Matter Learning: A Study of Sheltered Subject-Matter Classes at the University of Ottawa." *The Canadian Modern Language Review* 41:268–82.

Elbow, P. 1973. *Writing Without Teachers.* New York: Oxford University Press.

————. 1981. *Writing with Power.* New York: Oxford University Press.

Elley, W. 1991. "Acquiring Literacy in a Second Language: The Effect of Book-Based Programs." *Language Learning* 41 (3):375–411.

————. 1992. *How in the World Do Children Read?* Hamburg: International Association for the Evaluation of Educational Achievement.

————. 1998. *Raising Literacy Levels in Third World Countries: A Method That Works.* Culver City, CA: Language Education Associates.

Elley, W., and F. Mangubhai. 1983. "The Impact of Reading on Second Language Learning." *Reading Research Quarterly* 19:53–67.

Ellis, R. 1995. "Modified Oral Input and the Acquisition of Word Meanings." *Applied Linguistics* 16:409–41.

Ellis, R., Y. Tanaka, and A. Yamazaki. 1994. "Classroom Interaction, Comprehension, and L2 Vocabulary Acquisition." *Language Learning* 44:449–91.

Emery, C., and M. Csikszentmihalyi. 1982. "The Socialization Effects of Cultural Role Models in Ontogenetic Development and Upward Mobility." *Child Psychiatry and Human Development* 12:3–19.

Emig, J. 1971. *The Composing Processes of Twelfth Graders.* Urbana, IL: National Council of Teachers of English.

Faigley, L., and S. Witte. 1981. "Analyzing Revision." *College Composition and Communication* 32:400–14.

Fazio, L. 2001. "The Effect of Corrections and Commentaries of the Journal Writing Accuracy of Minority- and Majority-Language Students." *Journal of Second Language Writing* 10 (4): 235–49.

Glueck, W., and L. Jauch. 1975. "Sources of Ideas Among Production Scholars." *Journal of Higher Education* 46:103–14.

Goertzel, M., V. Goertzel, and T. Goertzel. 1978. *Three Hundred Eminent Personalities.* San Francisco: Jossey-Bass.

Greaney, V., and M. Clarke. 1973. "A Longitudinal Study of the Effects of Two Reading Methods on Leisure-Time Reading Habits." In *Reading: What of the Future?* edited by D. Moyle, 107–14. London: United Kingdom Reading Association.

Gruber, H. 1995. "Insight and Affect in the History of Science." In *The Nature of Insight,* edited by R. Steinberg and J. Davidson, 397–431. Cambridge, MA: MIT Press.

Hammond, R. 1988. "Accuracy Versus Communicative Competency: The Acquisition of Grammar in the Second Language Classroom." *Hispania* 71:408–17.

Harley, B. 1987. "Functional Grammar in French Immersion: A Classroom Experiment." *Applied Linguistics* 10:331–59.

Hauptman, P., M. Wesche, and D. Ready. 1988. "Second-Language Acquisition Through Subject Matter Learning: A Follow-Up Study at the University of Ottawa." *Language Learning* 38:433–71.

Hayes, D., and M. Ahrens. 1988. "Vocabulary Simplification for Children: A Special Case of 'motherese'?" *Journal of Child Language* 15:395–410.

Hemingway, E. 1997 [1927]. *Men Without Women.* New York: Scribner.

Herda, R., and F. Ramos. 2001. "How Consistently Do Students Read During Sustained Silent Reading?" *California School Library Journal,* 24 (2):29–31.

Horst, M., T. Cobb, and P. Meara. 1998. "Beyond a Clockwork Orange: Acquiring Second Language Vocabulary Through Reading." *Reading in a Foreign Language,* 11 (2):207–23.

Hulstijn, J., and W. Hulstijn. 1984. "Grammatical Errors as a Function of Processing Contraints and Explicit Knowledge." *Language Learning* 34:23–43.

Hyde, T., and J. Jenkins. 1969. "Differential Effects of Incidental Tasks on the Organization of Recall of a List of Highly Associated Words." *Journal of Experimental Psychology* 82:472–81.

Isik, A. 2000. "The Role of Input in Second Language Acquisition: More Comprehensible Input Supported by Grammar Instruction or More Grammar Instruction?" *ITL: Review of Applied Linguistics* 129–130:225–74.

Jafarpur, A., and M. Yamimi. 1993. "Does Practice with Dictation Improve Language Skills?" *System* 21 (3):359–69.

Jourdenais, R., M. Ota, S. Stauffer, B. Boyson, and C. Doughty. 1995. "Does Textual Enhancement Promote Noticing? A Think-Aloud Protocol Analysis." In *Attention and Awareness in Foreign Language Learning,* edited by R. Schmidt, 183–216. Honolulu, HI: University of Hawaii, Second Language Teaching and Curriculum Center.

Kim, H., and S. Krashen, 1998a. "The Author and Magazine Recognition Tests as Predictors of Literacy Development in Korean." *Perceptual and Motor Skills* 87:1376–78.

———. 1998b. "The Author Recognition and Magazine Recognition Tests, and Free Voluntary Reading as Predictors of Vocabulary Development in English as a Foreign Language for Korean High School Students." *System* 26:515–23.

Kim, J., and S. Krashen. 2000. "Another Home Run." *California English* 6 (2):25.

Kitajima, R. 2001. "The Effect of Instructional Conditions on Students' Vocabulary Retention." *Foreign Language Annals,* 34 (5):470–82.

Kohn, A. 1993. *Punished by Rewards.* Boston: Houghton Mifflin.

Krashen, S. 1981. *Second Language Acquisition and Second Language Learning.* New York: Prentice-Hall.

————. 1982. *Principles and Practice in Second Language Acquisition*. New York: Prentice-Hall.

————. 1985. *The Input Hypothesis: Issues and Implications*. Beverly Hills, CA: Laredo.

————. 1989. "We Acquire Vocabulary and Spelling by Reading: Additional Evidence for the Input Hypothesis." *Modern Language Journal* 73:440–64.

————. 1990. "How Reading and Writing Make You Smarter, or, How Smart People Read and Write." In *Georgetown Round Table on Languages and Linguistics*, edited by J. Alatis, 364–76. Washington, DC: Georgetown University Press.

————. 1991. "Sheltered Subject Matter Teaching." *Cross Currents* 18:183–88. Reprinted in *Methods That Work*, edited by J. Oller, 143–48. Boston: Heinle and Heinle.

————. 1992. "Under What Conditions, If Any, Should Formal Grammar Instruction Take Place?" *TESOL Quarterly* 26:409–11.

————. 1993a. "The Effect of Formal Grammar Study: Still Peripheral." *TESOL Quarterly* 27:722–25.

————. 1993b. *The Power of Reading*. Englewood, CO: Libraries Unlimited.

————. 1994a. "The Input Hypothesis and Its Rivals." In *Implicit and Explicit Learning of Languages*, edited by N. Ellis, 45–77. London: Academic Press.

————. 1994b. "The Pleasure Hypothesis." In *Georgetown University Round Table on Languages and Linguistics*, edited by J. Alatis, 299–322. Washington, DC: Georgetown University Press.

————. 1996. *Under Attack: The Case Against Bilingual Education*. Culver City, CA: Language Education Associates.

————. 1998. "Comprehensible Output?" *System* 26:175–82.

————. 1999a. *Three Arguments Against Whole Language and Why They Are Wrong*. Portsmouth, NH: Heinemann.

————. 1999b. "Seeking a Role for Grammar: A Review of Some Recent Studies." *Foreign Language Annals*, 32 (2):245–57.

————. 2001. "More Smoke and Mirrors: A Critique of the National Reading Panel (NRP) Report on 'Fluency.'" *Phi Delta Kappan* 83 (2):119–23.

————. 2002. "Optimal Levels of Writing Management: A Re-analysis of Boice." *Education* 122 (3):605–8.

Krashen, S., and T. Terrell. 1983. *The Natural Approach: Language Acquisition in the Classroom*. New York: Prentice-Hall.

Krashen, S., and D. Von Sprecken. 2002. "Is There a Decline in the Reading Romance?" *Knowledge Quest* 30 (3):11–17.

Ladas, H. 1980. "Summarizing Research: A Case Study." *Review of Educational Research* 50:597–624.

Lafayette, R., and M. Buscaglia. 1985. "Students Learn Language Via a Civilization Course—a Comparison of Second Language Acquisition Environments." *Studies in Second Language Acquisition* 7:323–42.

Lalande, J. 1982. "Reducing Composition Errors: An Experiment." *Modern Language Journal* 66 (2):140–49.

Lambert, W., and G. R. Tucker. 1972. *The Bilingual Education of Children*. New York: Newbury House.

Lamme, L. 1974. "Authors Popular Among Fifth Graders." *Elementary English* 51:1008–09.

Langer, J., and A. Applebee. 1987. *How Writing Shapes Thinking*. Urbana, IL: National Council of Teachers of English.

Lao, C.Y., and S. Krashen. 2000. "The Impact of Popular Literature Study on Literacy Development in EFL: More Evidence for the Power of Reading." *System* 28:261–70.

Lee, S-Y., and S. Krashen. 1996. "Free Voluntary Reading and Writing Competence in Taiwanese High School Students." *Perceptual and Motor Skills* 83:687–90.

Lee, S-Y., S. Krashen, and L. Tse. 1997. "The Author Recognition Test and Vocabulary Knowledge: A Replication." *Perceptual and Motor Skills* 83:648–50.

Lee, S-Y., and S. Krashen. 1997. "Writing Apprehension in Chinese as a First Language." *ITL: Review of Applied Linguistics* 115–116:27–37.

Lee, Y.O., S. Krashen, and B. Gribbons. 1996. "The Effect of Reading on the Acquisition of English Relative Clauses." *ITL: Review of Applied Linguistics* 113–114:263–73.

Leeman, J., I. Aregagoitia, D. Fridman, and C. Doughty. 1995. "Integrating Attention to Form with Meaning: Focus on Form in Content-Based Spanish Instruction." In *Attention and Awareness in Foreign Language Learning*, edited by R. Schmidt, 217–58. Honolulu, HI: University of Hawaii Press.

Lightbown, P., and M. Pienemann. 1993. "Comments on Stephen D. Krashen's 'Teaching Issues: Formal Grammar Instruction.'" *TESOL Quarterly* 27:717–22.

Loughrin-Sacco, S. 1992. "More Than Meets the Eye: An Ethnography of an Elementary French Class." *Canadian Modern Language Review* 49:80–101.

Lyster, R. 1994. "The Effect of Functional-Analytic Teaching on Aspects of French Immersion Students' Sociolinguistic Competence." *Applied Linguistics* 15 (3):263–87.

Lyster, R., and L. Ranta. 1997. "Corrective Feedback and Learner Uptake: Negotiation of Form in Communicative Classrooms." *Studies in Second Language Acquisition* 19: 37–66.

Mackey, A., and J. Philip. 1998. "Conversational Interaction and Second Language Development: Recasts, Responses, and Red Herrings?" *Modern Language Journal* 82 (3):338–56.

Manley, J., and L. Calk. 1997. "Grammar Instruction for Writing Skills: Do Students Perceive Grammar as Useful?" *Foreign Language Annals* 30:73–81.

Mason, B., and S. Krashen. 1997. "Extensive Reading in English as a Foreign Language." *System* 25:91–102.

Master, P. 1994. "The Effect of Systematic Instruction on Learning the English Article System." In *Perspectives on Pedagogical Grammar*, edited by T. Odlin, 229–52. Cambridge: Cambridge University Press.

Massimini, F., M. Csikszentmihalyi, and A. Della Fave. 1992. "Flow and Biocultural Evolution." In *Optimal Experience: Psychological Studies of Flow in Consciousness*, edited by M. Csikszentmihalyi and I. Csikszentmihalyi, 60–81 Cambridge: Cambridge University Press.

McQuillan, J. 1997. "The Effects of Incentives on Reading." *Reading Research and Instruction* 36:111–25.

Murray, D. 1990. *Shoptalk: Learning to Write with Writers*. Portsmouth, NH: Boynton/Cook.

Nagata, N. 1997. "An Experimental Comparison of Deductive and Inductive Feedback Generated by a Simple Parser." *System* 25:515–34.

Nagy, W., P. Herman, and R. Anderson. 1985. "Learning Words from Context." *Reading Research Quarterly* 20:233–53.

National Reading Panel. 2000. "Report of the National Reading Panel: Teaching Children to Read." Washington, DC: National Institutes of Health, NIH Publication No. 00-4754. Available from *www.nichd.nih.gov/publications/nrp/smallbook.pdf.*

Nell, V. 1988. *Lost in a Book.* New Haven, CT: Yale University Press.

Newmark, L. 1966. "How Not to Interfere with Language Learning." *International Journal of American Linguistics* 40:77–83.

Nicola, M. 1990. "Experimenting with the New Methods." *Dialog on Language Instruction* 6 (1, 2):61–72.

Nikolov, M., and S. Krashen. 1997. "Need We Sacrifice Accuracy for Fluency?" *System* 25:197–201.

Nobuyoshi, J., and R. Ellis. 1993. "Focused Communication Tasks and Second Language Acquisition." *ELT Journal* 47:203–10.

Norris, J., and L. Ortega. 2000. "Effectiveness of L2 Instruction: A Research Synthesis and Quantitative Meta-Analysis." *Language Learning* 50 (3):417–28.

Peper, R., and R. Meyer. 1986. "Generative Effects of Note-Taking During Science Lectures." *Journal of Educational Psychology* 78:34–38.

Pica, T. 1988. "Interactive Adjustments as an Outcome of NS-NNS Negotiated Interaction." *Language Learning* 38:45–73.

Pica, T., L. Holliday, N. Lewis, and L. Morgenthaler. 1989. "Comprehensible Output as an Outcome of Linguistic Demands on the Learner." *Studies in Second Language Acquisition* 11:63–90.

Pilgreen, J. 2000. *The SSR Handbook: How to Organize and Maintain a Sustained Silent Reading Program.* Portsmouth, NH: Heinemann.

Pilgreen, J., and S. Krashen. 1993. "Sustained Silent Reading with ESL High School Students: Impact on Reading Comprehension, Reading Frequency, and Reading Enjoyment." *School Library Media Quarterly* 22:21–23.

Pitts, M., H. White, and S. Krashen. 1989. "Acquiring Second Language Vocabulary Through Reading: A Replication of the Clockwork Orange Study Using Second Language Acquirers." *Reading in a Foreign Language* 5:271–75.

Price, M. 1991. "The Subjective Experience of Foreign Language Anxiety: Interviews with Highly Anxious Students." In *Language Anxiety,* edited by E. Horwitz and D. Young, 101–08. Englewood Cliffs, NJ: Prentice-Hall.

Ramos, F., and S. Krashen. 1998. "The Impact of One Trip to the Public Library: Making Books Available May Be the Best Incentive for Reading." *The Reading Teacher* 51 (7):614–15.

Ravitch, D., and C. Finn. 1987. *What Do Our 17-Year-Olds Know?* New York: Harper and Row.

Robb, T., S. Ross, and I. Shortreed. 1986. "Salience of Feedback on Error and Its Effects on ESL Writing Quality." *TESOL Quarterly* 13:145–38.

Robinson, P. 1995. "Aptitude, Awareness, and the Fundamental Similarity of Implicit and Explicit Second Language Learning." In *Attention and Awareness in Foreign Language Learning,* edited by R. Schmidt, 303–57. Honolulu, HI: University of Hawaii Press.

————. 1997. "Generalizability and Automaticity of Second Language Learning Under Implicit, Incidental, Enhanced, and Instructed Conditions." *Studies in Second Language Acquisition* 19:223–47.

Rodrigo, V., J. McQuillan, and S. Krashen. 1996. "Free Voluntary Reading and Vocabulary Knowledge in Native Speakers of Spanish." *Perceptual and Motor Skills* 83:648–50.

Romney, J. C., D. Romney, and H. Menzies. 1995."Reading for Pleasure in French: A Study of the Reading Habits and Interests of French Immersion Children." *Canadian Modern Language Review* 51:474–511.

Rose, M. 1984. *Writer's Block: The Cognitive Dimension.* Carbondale, IL: Southern Illinois University Press.

Salaberry, M. R. 1997. "The Role of Input and Output Practice in Second Language Acquisition." *Canadian Modern Language Review* 53 (2):422–51.

Sato, I. 1992. "Bosozuku: Flow in Japanese Motorcycle Gangs." In *Optimal Experience: Psychological Studies of Flow in Consciousness,* edited by M. Csikszentmihalyi and I. Csikszentmihalyi, 92–117. Cambridge: Cambridge University Press.

Schaefer, C., and A. Anastasi. 1968. "A Biographical Inventory for Identifying Creativity in Adolescent Boys." *Journal of Applied Psychology* 58:42–48.

Scott, V., and S. Randall. 1992. "Can Students Apply Grammar Rules for Reading Textbook Explanations?" *Foreign Language Annals* 25:357–67.

Segal, J. 1997. "Summer Daze." Class paper, Trenton State University, summer.

Semke, H. 1984. "The Effects of the Red Pen." *Foreign Language Annals* 17:195–202.

Sheppard, K. 1992. "Two Feedback Types: Do They Make a Difference?" *RELC Journal,* 23 (1):103–10.

Shin, F. 2001. "Motivating Students with Goosebumps and Other Popular Books." *CSLA Journal* (California School Library Association) 25 (1):15–19.

Simonton, D. 1984. *Genius, Creativity, and Leadership.* Cambridge, MA: Harvard University Press.

———. 1988. *Scientific Genius: A Psychology of Science.* Cambridge, MA: Harvard University Press.

Smith, F. 1975. *Comprehension and Learning.* New York: Holt, Rinehart & Winston.

———. 1986. *Insult to Intelligence.* Portsmouth, NH: Heinemann.

———. 1988. *Joining the Literacy Club.* Portsmouth, NH: Heinemann.

———. 1994. *Writing and the Writer.* 2^d edition. Hillsdale, NJ: Erlbaum.

———. 1996. *Between Hope and Havoc.* Portsmouth, NH: Heinemann.

Smith, R., and G. Supanich. 1984. *The Vocabulary Scores of Company Presidents.* Technical Report 1984-1. Chicago: Johnson O'Connor Research Foundation.

Sommers, N. 1980. "Revision Strategies of Student Writers and Experienced Adult Writers." *College Composition and Communication* 31:378–88.

Spada, N., and P. Lightbown. 1993. "Instruction and the Development of Questions in L2 Classrooms." *Studies in Second Language Acquisition* 15 (2):205–21.

Stanovich, K., and A. Cunningham. 1992. "Studying the Consequences of Literacy Within a Literate Society: The Cognitive Correlates of Print Exposure." *Memory and Cognition* 20 (1):51–68.

———. 1993. "Where Does Knowledge Come From? Specific Associations Between Print Exposure and Information Acquisition." *Journal of Educational Psychology* 85 (2):211–29.

Stanovich, K., and R. West. 1989. "Exposure to Print and Orthographic Processing." *Reading Research Quarterly* 24:402–33.

Stanovich, K., R. West, and M. Harrison. 1995. "Knowledge Growth and Maintenance Across the Life Span: The Role of Print Exposure." *Developmental Psychology* 31 (5):811–26.

Sternfeld, S. 1992. "An Experiment in Foreign Language Education: The University of Utah's Immersion/Multiliteracy Program." In *Comprehension-Based Language Teaching*, edited by R. Chourchene, J. Glidden, and J. St. John, 407–32. Ottawa: University of Ottawa Press.

Stokes, J., S. Krashen, and J. Kartchner. 1998. "Factors in the Acquisition of the Present Subjunctive in Spanish: The Role of Reading and Study." *ITL: Review of Applied Linguistics* 121–122:19–25.

Swaffer, J., and M. Woodruff. 1978. "Language for Comprehension: Focus on Reading." *Modern Language Journal* 62:27–32.

Swain, M. 1985. "Communicative Competence: Some Roles of Comprehensible Input and Comprehensible Output in Its Development." In *Input in Second Language Acquisition*, edited by S. Gass and C. Madden, 235–56. New York: Newbury House.

———. 1995. "Three Functions of Output in Second Language Learning." In *Principle and Practice in Applied Linguistics: Studies in Honor of H.G. Widdowson*, edited by G. Cook and B. Seidelhofer, 125–44. Oxford: Oxford University Press.

Swain, M., and S. Lapkin. 1995. "Problems in Output and the Cognitive Processes They Generate: A Step Towards Second Language Learning." *Applied Linguistics* 16:371–91.

Sze, V. W. 1999. "Promoting Second Language Development and Reading Habits Through an Extensive Reading Scheme." In *Language Instructional Issues in Asian Classrooms*, edited by C.Y. Mee and N.S. Moi. Newark, DE: International Reading Association.

Tarone, E., and Liu, G-Q. 1995. "Situational Context, Variation, and Second Language Acquisition Theory." In *Principle and Practice in Applied Linguistics: Studies in Honor of H. G. Widdowson*, edited by G. Cook and B. Seidelhofer,107–24. Oxford: Oxford University Press.

Trelease, J. 2001. *The Read-Aloud Handbook.* 4th rev. ed. New York: Penguin.

Truscott, J. 1996. "The Case Against Grammar Correction in L2 Writing Classes." *Language Learning* 46 (2):327–69.

Tse, L. 1996. "When an ESL Adult Becomes a Reader." *Reading Horizons* 31 (1):16–29.

Van den Branden, K. 1997. "Effects of Negotiation on Language Learners' Output." *Language Learning* 47:589–636.

Van Zelst, R., and W. Kerr. 1951. "Some Correlates of Technical and Scientific Productivity." *Journal of Abnormal Psychology* 46:470–75.

VanPatten, B., and T. Cadierno. 1993. "Explicit Instruction and Input Processing." *Studies in Second Language Acquisition* 15:225–41.

VanPatten, B., and C. Sanz. 1995. "From Input to Output: Processing Instruction and Communicative Tasks." In *Second Language Acquisition Theory and Pedagogy*, edited by F. Eckman, D. Highland, P. Lee, J. Milcham, and R. Weber, 169–85. Mahwah, NJ: Erlbaum.

Von Sprecken, D., J. Kim, and S. Krashen. 2000. "The Home Run Book: Can One Positive Reading Experience Create a Reader?" *California School Library Journal* 23 (2):8–9.

Von Sprecken, D., and S. Krashen. 1998. Do Students Read During Sustained Silent Reading?" California Reader 32 (1):11–13.

Wallace, I., and J. Pear. 1977. "Self-Control Techniques of Famous Novelists." *Journal of Applied Behavior Analysis* 10:515–25.

Wallas, G. 1926. *The Art of Thought.* London: C. A. Watts. Quoted in *Creativity*, edited by P.E. Vernon, 1970, 91–97. Middlesex, England: Penguin.

Walsh, D., and J. Jenkins. 1973. "Effects of Orienting Tasks on Free Recall in Incidental Learning: 'Difficulty,' 'Effort,' and 'Process' Explanations." *Journal of Verbal Learning and Verbal Behavior* 12:481–88.

West, R., and K. Stanovich. 1991. "The Incidental Acquisition of Information from Reading." *Psychological Science* 2:325–30.

West, R., K. Stanovich, and H. Mitchell. 1993. "Reading in the Real World and Its Correlates." *Reading Research Quarterly* 28:35–50.

Wheldall, K., and J. Entwhistle. 1988. "Back in the USSR: The Effect of Teacher Modeling of Silent Reading on Pupils' Reading Behaviour in the Primary School Classroom." *Educational Psychology* 8:51–56.

White, L. 1991. "Adverb Placement in Second Language Acquisition: Some Effects of Positive and Negative Evidence in the Classroom." *Second Language Research* 7:133–61.

White, L., N. Spada, P. Lightbown, and L. Ranta. 1991. "Input Enhancement and L2 Question Formation." *Applied Linguistics* 12:416–32.

Winitz, H. 1996. "Grammaticality Judgments as a Function of Explicit and Implicit Instruction in Spanish." *Modern Language Journal* 80 (1):32–46.

Winokur, J. 1990. *Writers on Writing.* Philadelphia: Running Press.

Wolfe, D., and G. Jones. 1982. "Integrating Total Physical Response Strategy in a Level I Spanish Class." *Foreign Language Annals* 14 (4):273–80.

Yang, A. 2001. "Reading and the Non-academic Learner: A Mystery Solved." *System* 29 (4):451–66.

Yang, L., and T. Givon. 1997. "Benefits and Drawbacks of Controlled Laboratory Studies of Second Language Acquisition." *Studies in Second Language Acquisition* 19:173–93.

Young, D. 1990. "An Investigation of Students' Perspectives on Anxiety and Speaking." *Foreign Language Annals* 23:539–53.

Index

academic language, 12–13
acquisition-learning hypothesis, 1, 58
adult students, sheltered subject-matter
    teaching of, 13
affective filter hypothesis, 6
age, work quality and, 75
Ahrens, M., 22
Alanen, R., 39–40, 41, 42
Altos test of reading comprehension and
    vocabulary, 20
Anastasi, A., 72
Anderson, R., 62
anxiety, speaking and, 63–64
Applebee, A., 74
Aregagoitia, I., 33–34
arousal, in reading, 23
artificial language, 57
Art of Thought, The (Wallas), 68
Asher, James, 4, 9–10, 14*n*.2, 83
authors
    named by immersion students, 65
    recognition test, 21–22

Baretta, A., 14*n*.2
bedtime reading, 23
binge writing, 76
Black Stallion, The, series, 26
Bloom, B., 80
Boice, Robert, *viii*, 75–76, 76, 81–82,
    81*n*.7
books. *See also* reading material
    discussions, 25
    handcrafted, 25–26
    recommendations, 25
Boyson, B., 53–54
Bransford, J., 71
Brazerman, C., 73
Brown, M., 8
Burling, Robins, 4
Burnett, C., 79, 80
Buscaglia, M., 13, 14

Calk, L., 38–39, 41, 42
Cho, K. S., 16, 24
Chomsky, N., 6
Clark, R., 69
Clarke, M., 24
Cobb, T., 28*n*.2, 29*n*.3
cognitive development. *See also* creativity;
    idea creation
    assigned reading and, 73
    problem solving and, 72–78, 84–85
    reading and, 72–73, 78–79
    school assumptions about, 85
    writing and, 73–77, 78–79
Cohen, Y., 17, 25
communicative tests, 83
competence, fading, 42–43, 45
composition. *See* writing
comprehensible input-based methods, 83.
    See also input (comprehension)
        hypothesis
    effectiveness of, 8–12
    grammar study *vs.*, 10–12
    skill-building *vs.*, 8–10
    value of, 83, 84
comprehensible output (CO) hypothesis,
    vii–viii, 59–65
    acquisition without output, 62
    defined, 59
    discomfort of, 63–64
    input hypothesis *vs.*, 66*n*.4
    interaction hypothesis and, 64
    language acquisition and, 62–63
    need hypothesis and, 64–65
    problems of, 65
    scarcity argument, 60–61
comprehension
    computer-based evaluation, 50–51
    free reading and, 19
    grammar instruction and, 40
Comprehension and Learning (Smith),
    68

97

comprehension hypothesis, 4. *See also* input (comprehension) hypothesis
computer reading evaluation, 50–51
Condon, Richard, 77
conscious learning
  acquisition *vs.*, 35–36
  competence fading, 42–43, 45
  defined, 1
  effectiveness of, 41, 44–45
  form focus and, 67n.4
  free-response measures, 59
  limits of, 32–33
  Monitor hypothesis and, 2, 44
Constantino, R., 16, 17n
constrained response, 58
continuation studies, 13–14
"cooking," 68
core reading, 73
creativity
  age and, 75
  idea generation process, 68–70
  reading and, 72
  writing and, 75–77
Csikszentmihalyi, M., 23, 69, 72
cultural knowledge, 72
Cumming, A., 61
Cunningham, A., 72, 81, 81n.4

Danskin, D., 79, 80
Day, E., 43, 45, 49–50, 59
deductive grammar learning, 30
Defense Language Institute, 10
De Graaff, R., 37–38, 41, 42
delayed tests. *See also* posttests
  competence fading measured by, 42–43, 45
  foreign language immersion student performance on, 46–48
direct grammar instruction. *See also* grammar instruction
  defined, 30
  effectiveness of, 41–42, 44–45, 49–50, 83–84
  free-response evaluation, 49–50
  oral communication tasks and, 48–49
Doughty, C., 33–34, 45, 50–51, 53–54
Dupuy, B., 62

effect size, in free response tests, 56, 59, 66n.2
EFL students, comprehensible output hypothesis and, 60
Einstein, Albert, 69, 75
Elbow, P., 68, 78
Elley, W., 18–19, 83
Ellis, R., 60, 62, 64, 66n.3
Emery, C., 72
enterprises, 78–79
error correction
  free-response tests, 52–53
  learning and, 1
  self-correction, 2
ESL students, grammar instruction effectiveness, 31–33, 34–37, 48–49
"explicit grammar" approach, 11. *See also* direct grammar instruction
extensive reading programs
  accountability in, 18
  defined, 18
  effectiveness of, 19, 26–28n.1

Faigley, L., 76
Fear Street series, 26
feedback, comprehensible output hypothesis and, 61
Feynman, Richard, 80, 80n.1
fill-in-the-blank tests, 56–57
Finn, C., 72
first-language acquisition order, 2
flow
  in reading, 23
  in writing, 76–77
follow-up tests, 57. *See also* delayed tests
forced writing, 82n.7
Foreign Language Annals, viii
foreign language students
  author recognition test performance, 21
  free-response evaluation, 46–48, 49–50, 54–55
  grammar instruction research, 33–34, 38–40
  Handcrafted Books for, 25–26
  performance evaluation, 53–54
form focus
  direct grammar instruction and, 33, 49–50, 53–54, 83
  free-response tests, 56, 57, 58–59
  learning and, 67n.4

in oral communication tasks, 48
posttest evaluation, 45
free-response tests, 44–59
  error correction, 52–53
  foreign language students, 46–48, 49–50,
    54–55
  grammar instruction effectiveness and,
    44–59
  immersion program students, 51–52
  information-gap activities, 52–53
  performance evaluation, 53–54
  on reading passages, 50–51
  research summary, 58–59
  storytelling, 55
free voluntary reading, 15–29
  author recognition test and, 21–22
  case histories on, 16–18
  correlational studies on, 15–16
  effectiveness of, 18–20
  in-school, 18–20
  research on, 15–22
  value of, 15, 22, 79
frequent words, 22
Fridman, D., 33–34

Givon, T., 45, 57
Glueck, W., 81, 81n.5
Goertzel, M., 72
Goertzel, T., 72
Goertzel, V., 72
Goodman, Kenneth, 4
Goosebumps series, 20, 26
"grammar audio-lingual" methodology,
  10–11
grammar instruction, 30–59
  competence fading, 42–43, 45
  comprehensible input-based methods vs.,
    8–10, 10–12
  defined, 30
  direct, 30
  effectiveness of, 5–6, 31–45, 49–50, 83–84
  for ESL students, 31–33, 48–49
  experimental studies, 31–42
  explicit, 38
  focus on form, 33–34
  foreign language immersion student
    performance and, 46–48
  free-response tests and, 44–59
  implicit vs. explicit approach, 11, 43

incidental, 37
long-term effects of, 42–43, 44, 45, 57
oral communication tasks and, 48–49
peripheral effects of, 30
posttest measurements of effectiveness,
  42–43, 45
research characteristics, 32
role of, 8, 30–59
second-language competence and, vii
Total Physical Response (TPR) method vs.,
  9–10
grammar learning. See also learning
  conscious learning, 32–33
  deductive, 30
  inductive rule learning (rule search), 30
grammaticality judgments, 36–38, 40, 58
Greaney, V., 24
Gribbons, B., 15, 16n
Gruber, H., 80, 80n.1

Hammond, R., 10, 83
Handcrafted Books, 25–26
Harley, B., 43, 45, 46–48, 59
Hayes, D., 22
Helmholz, Hermann, 69
Hemingway, Ernest, 3
Herda, R., 25
Herman, P., 62
high achievers, 69–70
Holes, 20
Horst, M., 28n.2, 29n.3
How Writers Journey to Comfort and Fluency
  (Boice), viii
Hyde, T., 71

idea creation. See also creativity; problem
  solving
  process of, 68–70
  writing and, 75–77
illumination stage, in idea generation, 68,
  70, 77
immersion instruction
  comprehensible output hypothesis and,
    61, 65
  free-response testing, 51–52
  grammar instruction effectiveness, 46–48
  "immersion multiliteracy" programs, 14
implicit learning, 11, 34, 41
incidental learning, 71

incubation stage, in idea generation, 68
  breaks, 80n.1
  characteristics of, 69–70
  reading and, 72
  scheduling, 70
  writing and, 73–74, 76
inductive rule learning, 30. *See also* rule
  search
"industrious passive reading," 72
information-gap activities, 52–53
input (comprehension) hypothesis, *vii*.
  See also comprehensible input-based
  methods
  cognitive development and, 84
  corollaries of, 5–6
  defined, 4
  natural order hypothesis and, 4
  output hypothesis *vs.*, 66n.4
in-school free reading, 18–20, 28n.1. *See also*
  free voluntary reading
inspiration, writing and, 76
interaction hypothesis, 64
interaction-modified input, 60
international students, free reading by, 15–16
Isik, A., 11–12, 83
Island of the Blue Dolphins, The, 20

Jauch, L., 81, 81n.5
Jenkins, J., 71
Jourdenais, R., 45, 53–54

Kartchner, J., 15, 16, 16n
Kerr, W., 72
Keillor, Garrison, 64
Kim, J., 24
Kitajima, R., 66n.4, 67n.5
knowledge, reading and, 23, 72–73, 81n.4
Kohn, Alfie, 85
Krashen, S., 10, 11, 13, 14n.2, 15, 16, 16n, 18,
  19, 22, 23, 24, 25, 26, 28n.1, 30, 44, 48,
  62, 65, 67n.4, 78, 83
Kusudo, J., 9–10

Ladas, H., 73
Lafayette, R., 13, 14
Langer, J., 74
language acquisition
  anxiety and, 63–64
  characteristics of, 4
  conscious learning *vs.*, 35–36
  defined, 1
  direct instruction and, 52
  grammar instruction and, *vii*
  predictable order of, 1–2
  principles of, 1–14
  reading and, 78–79
  speaking and, 5, 8
  without output, 62
  writing and, 78–79
"language acquisition device," 6
language acquisition theory. *See also* specific
  hypotheses
  acquisition-learning hypothesis, 1, 58
  affective filter hypothesis, 6
  comprehensible input hypothesis, *vii*
  comprehensible output theory and,
    vii–viii, 59–60, 59–65, 62–63
  hypotheses, *vii*, 1–6
  input (comprehension) hypothesis, *vii*,
    5–6
  interaction hypothesis, 64
  Monitor hypothesis, 3–4, 31, 40, 44, 48,
    55–56, 58
  natural order hypothesis, 1–2, 4
  need hypothesis, 64–65
  pleasure hypothesis, 22–23
language classes
  beginning level, 7–8
  characteristics of, 7–8
  effectiveness of, 6–7
  goals of, 7
language learning, 1
Lao, C. Y., 19, 26, 28n.1
Lapkin, S., 61
learning. *See also* conscious learning
  implicit, 11, 34, 41
  incidental, 71
  intentional, 71
  problem solving and, 80n.2
  relevance and, 71
  school assumptions about, 85
  school reading assignments and, 73
  through problem solving, 70–71
Lee, C. Y., 23
Lee, Sy-ying, *viii*
Lee, Y. O., 15, 16n
Leeman, J., 33–34, 41
library visits, 24

Lightbown, P., 43, 48, 65*n*.1
light reading ,value of, 22, 26
Liu, G-Q, 63
Loughrin-Sacco, S., 63–64
Lyster, R., 45, 51–52, 58–59, 61

Mackey, A., 45, 52–53
Malcolm X, 62
Mangubhai, F., 18–19, 83
Manley, J., 38–39, 41, 42
Mason, B., 19
Master, P., 31–33, 41
Maugham, W. Somerset, 23
Mayer of Casterbridge, The, 28*n*.2
Meaning-Oriented Group (MOG),
    50–51
Meara, P., 28*n*.2, 29*n*.3
Men Without Women (Hemingway), 3
Menzies, H., 65
Mitchell, H., 21
Monitor hypothesis
    conditions for using Monitor, 3, 44, 48, 58,
        67n.4, 83
    conscious learning and, 2
    defined, 2–3
    free-response tests, 55–56
    grammar instruction and, 31,
        40, 44
    "over-Monitoring," 3
motivation
    for reading, 24–25
    school assumptions about, 85

Nagata, N., 45, 56–57
Nagy, W., 62
Nancy Drew series, 26
National Reading Panel (NRP), 18
National Taipei University, Taiwan, *vii*
Natural Approach, 8, 10, 12, 84
natural order hypothesis, 1–2, 4
need hypothesis, 64–65
Nell, V., 23
Nelson-Denny reading comprehension test,
    20
Nicola, M., 10
Nikolov, M., 11, 83
Nobuyoshi, J., 62
Norris, J., 43, 44, 46, 54, 58, 59,
    66*n*.2

omnivorous readers, 72
oral language. *See also* speaking
    free-response tests, 48–49, 59
    problem solving through, 77–78
Ortega, L., 43, 44, 46, 54, 58, 59, 66*n*.2
Ota, M., 53–54
output-based activities, 66*n*.4. *See also*
    comprehensible output (CO)
    hypothesis

Palmer, A., 8
Pauling, Linus, 71
peripheral reading, 73
Philip, J., 45, 52–53
Piaget, J., 80, 80*n*.1
Pica, T., 60
Pienemann, M., 48
Pitts, M., 62
pleasure hypothesis, 22–23
pleasure reading, 22–23, 65
popular literature
    reading progress and, 20
    series books, 16–17, 20, 26
    sheltered, 26
posttests. *See also* delayed tests
    competence fading measured by, 42–43, 45
    foreign language immersion student
        performance on, 46–48
    free-response tests, 57
Prairie Home Companion, 64
premodified input, 60
preparation stage, in idea generation, 68
Price, M., 64
print environment
    cognitive development and, 72–73
    comprehensible input hypothesis and, 84
    exposure measures, 80*n*.2
problem solving
    cognitive development and, 72–78, 84–85
    idea generation process, 68–70
    learning and, 70–71, 80*n*.2
    student success in, 80
    through oral language, 77–78
    through writing, 74, 76–77
productivity, writing and, 74–75

Ramos, F., 24, 25
Randall, S., 42–43
Ranta, L., 48, 61

Ravitch, D., 72
read-alouds, 25
reading
  author recognition test and, 21
  at bedtime, 23
  cognitive development and, 72–73
  comprehension, 21
  computer-based evaluation, 50–51
  core, 73
  creativity and, 72
  cultural knowledge and, 72
  effects of positive experiences, 24–25
  as flow activity, 23
  free voluntary, 15–29
  light, 22
  modeling, 25
  motivation, 24–25
  overreading, 72
  peripheral, 73
  pleasure, 22–23
  providing time for, 25
  school assignments, 73
  selective, 73
  sustained silent reading, 83
  value of, 22–24, 71, 78–79
  volume of, 21
  writing competence and, 78
reading material. See also books
  library trips, 24
  recommending, 25
  relevancy of, 73
  variety of, 24–25
Reading-Oriented Group (ROG), 50–51
recreational reading. See free voluntary
    reading
relaxation, through reading, 23
relevance
  learning and, 71, 73
  of reading material, 73
Robinson, P., 34–37, 41, 42
Romney, D., 65
Romney, J. C., 65
rules
  competence fading effects, 43, 44
  composition errors, 39
  evaluation of use, 53–54
  free-response test performance, 46–59
  inductive (example-based) feedback, 56
  knowledge of, 3
  Monitor and, 3

rule-driven deductive feedback, 56–57
  test performance, 40
rule search
  defined, 30
  grammaticality judgment and, 37–38
  results of, 35

Salaberry, M. R., 45, 57–58
Sanz, C., 45, 54–56, 59
Sawyer, K., 69
Schaefer, C., 72
school
  enterprises in, 79
  incubation in, 77
  learning assumptions, 85
  reading assignments, 73
  writing purpose in, 77
Scott, V., 42–43
second-language acquisition. See also foreign
    language students
  grammar instruction and, vii
  Handcrafted Books for, 25–26
  order of, 2
Segal, J., 17
selected response, 58
selective reading, 73
self-correction. See also error correction
  Monitor hypothesis and, 2
sentence-completion tests, 40, 56–57, 58
series books
  Goosebumps series, 20, 26
  reading progress and, 26
  Sweet Valley High series, 16–17
Shapson, S., 43, 45, 49–50, 59
shared reading, 19
sheltered popular literature, 26
sheltered subject-matter teaching, 14, 84
  for intermediate level learners, 12–13
  research on, 13
Shin, F., 20
Simonton, D., 72, 75
skills focus, 83
Smith, Frank, 4, 44, 68, 71, 76, 78, 84, 85
Smith, R., 29n.3
Sommers, N., 76
Spada, N., 43, 48, 65n.1
speaking. See also oral language
  comprehensible output hypothesis and,
    60–61, 63–64, 65
  discomfort of, 63–64

language acquisition and, 5, 8
Monitor and, 3
spelling, 3, 21
"spontaneous communicative language,"
48–49
Stanovich, K., 21, 72, 80, 80n.3, 81, 81n.4
Stauffer, S., 53–54
Stokes, J., 15, 16, 16n
Stone, Irving, 77
storytelling, 55
study skills, 79–80
Supanich, G., 29n.3
sustained silent reading, 83
defined, 18
providing time for, 25
value of, 24, 28n.1
Swaffer, J., 13–14
Swain, Merrill, vii–viii, 60, 61, 63, 65
Sweet Valley High series, 16–17, 26
System, viii
Sze, V. W., 26

Tanaka, Y., 60, 62, 64, 66n.3
Tarone, E., 63
Terrell, T., 10
Test of English as a Foreign Language
(TOEFL), 16, 17
think-aloud procedures
comprehensible output hypothesis and, 61
performance evaluation, 54
writing and, 81n.6
thinking process, 68–69. See also cognitive
development
time pressure
grammaticality judgment task and, 38
test performance and, 41
Torre, R. de la, 9–10
Total Physical Response (TPR) method, 4, 7,
12, 14n.2, 84
grammar instruction vs., 9–10
translation tests, 56–57
Trelease, Jim, 24
Tse, L., 24
Tunis, John R. series, 26

uncommon words, 22
unmodified input, comprehensible output
hypothesis and, 60

Van den Branden, K., 60, 63
VanPatten, B., 45, 54–56, 57, 59

Van Zelst, R., 72
verification stage, in idea generation, 68
vocabulary
author recognition test and, 21
direct study of, 28n.2, 29n.3
free voluntary reading and, 16–17, 28n.2
reading effects on, 28n.2
tests, 28n.2
Von Sprecken, D., 25

Wallas, Graham, 68, 69–70, 72, 73, 77
West, R., 21, 72
What Do Our 17-Year-Olds Know? (Ravitch
and Finn), 72
White, H., 62
White, L., 45, 48
whole language, 83
Winitz, H., 4, 11, 83
Witte, S., 76
Woodruff, M., 13–14
words
frequent, 22
translation test, 40
uncommon, 22
Wright, Richard, 62
writer's block, 76–77
writing
author recognition test and, 21
binge, 76
cognitive development and, 73–77
composing process, 76–77
comprehensible output hypothesis and, 61
errors, 39
evaluation, 54
forced, 82n.7
free-response measures, 57
idea creation and, 75–77
illumination and, 77
inspiration and, 76
mechanics and, 76
problem-solving and, 74
reading and, 78
regularity of, 75–76
value of, 71, 74, 78–79
writing apprehension, 23

Yamazaki, A., 60, 62, 64, 66n.3
Yang, A., 27–28n.1
Yang, L., 45, 57
Young, D., 63–64

ARTHUR IN A PICKLE

酸黄瓜噩梦

（美）马克·布朗　绘著

范晓星　译

CHISO 新疆青少年出版社

The school bell rang.

"Time to hand in your homework,"

said Mister Ratburn.

Everyone did—but Arthur.

3

"Where is your homework?"

Mister Ratburn asked Arthur.

"My dog ate it," said Arthur.

"I don't think so,"

said Mister Ratburn.

"Go to the principal's office

first thing in the morning.

You're in a pickle now, Arthur."

5

That night, Arthur just played
with his food.

He tossed and turned in bed.
"I'm in a pickle," he said again
and again until he fell asleep.

Arthur dreamed that
the pickle police
were chasing him!

8

He jumped into his pickle car.

He stepped on the gas—

but he didn't get far.

The pickle police said,

"Take him away!"

Up in the sky, a pickle plane
flew through pickle snow
and rain.

10

The pilot threw down a rope
and pulled Arthur up.

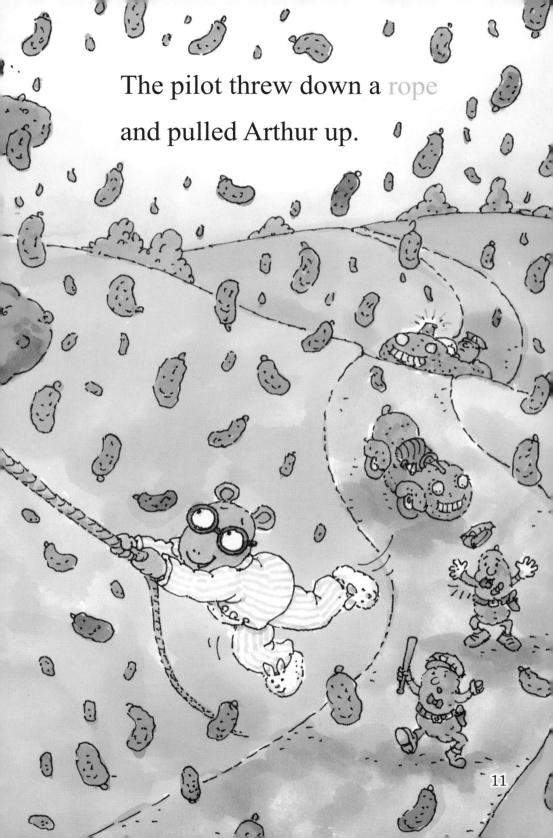

The plane went down
in Pickletown.

"Look!" said D.W. "A pickle steeple!"

"Look!" said Arthur. "Pickle people!"

13

Some had pickle hair.

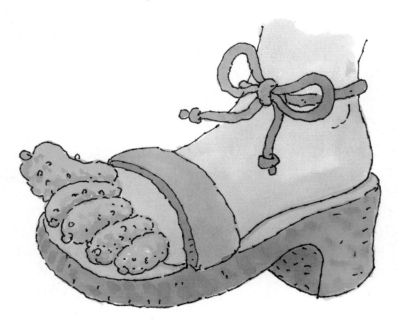

Some had pickle toes.

14

Some a pickle ear.

Some a pickle nose.

15

"Didn't do his homework!"
said Pickle Nose.

"Lied that he did!"
said Pickle Toes.

16

"You're going to jail—
and absolutely no bail!"
shouted Judge Picklepuss.

The jailer put Arthur

on a pickle diet,

and every day he said,

"Just try it."

For breakfast, pickle doughnuts
and pickle flakes…

For lunch, pickle pie
and pickle shakes…

For dinner, pickle soup
and pickle cakes.

"Let me out!

Don't be so mean.

I've had it," moaned Arthur.

"I'm turning green."

Suddenly, Arthur woke up.

He went to his desk,

opened his book,

and did his homework.

21

At school, Arthur went right
to the principal's office.
"I cannot tell a lie," he said.
"My dog did not eat
my homework.
I did not do my homework.
But here it is now.
I'm sorry."
The principal smiled.
"Well, thank you, Arthur,"
he said.

Arthur felt great all day—
until he asked,
"What's for dinner?"
and Dad said,
"Pickled cabbage!"

24

译文

2. 上课铃响了。
"该交作业了。"舒老师说。
大家都交了作业，只有亚瑟没交。

4. "你的作业呢？"舒老师问亚瑟。
5. "被我的小狗吃掉了。"亚瑟回答。
"怎么可能?"舒老师说,"明天一早先到校长办公室去。你可麻烦了，亚瑟。"

6. 晚上，亚瑟没心思吃饭。

26

7. 他在床上翻来覆去。

"我麻烦了。"亚瑟自言自语地说了一遍又一遍，才迷迷糊糊地睡着。

8. 亚瑟梦见一个酸黄瓜警察在后面追他！

9. 他跳上一辆酸黄瓜汽车，猛踩油门，可惜也没开出多远。

酸黄瓜警察说："把他带走！"

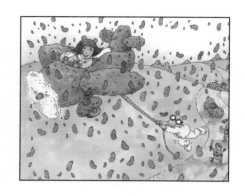

10. 这时候，天上下起酸黄瓜雨，一架酸黄瓜飞机开了过来。

11. 担任飞行员的朵拉扔下一根绳子，把亚瑟拉了上去。

12. 飞机在酸黄瓜镇降落。

13. "看！"朵拉说，"酸黄瓜屋顶！"

"看！"亚瑟说，"酸黄瓜人！"

14. 有人长着酸黄瓜头发。

有人长着酸黄瓜脚趾。

15. 有人长着酸黄瓜耳朵。

有人长着酸黄瓜鼻子。

16. "他没有写完作业！"酸黄瓜鼻子先生说。

"他说谎了！"酸黄瓜脚趾小姐说。

17. "我要把你送进监狱，不许保释！"酸黄瓜法官吼叫着说。

29

18. 监狱长天天给亚瑟吃用酸黄瓜做成的食物，每次他都说："尝尝看吧。"

19. 早餐是酸黄瓜面包圈和酸黄瓜麦片……

午餐是酸黄瓜馅儿饼和酸黄瓜奶昔……

晚餐是酸黄瓜汤和酸黄瓜蛋糕。

20. "放我出去！你们这些坏蛋！我受够了！"亚瑟大喊，"我都快变成酸黄瓜了！"

21. 突然，亚瑟醒了过来。

他走到书桌前，翻开书本，写起作业来。

22. 第二天一早，亚瑟来到校长办公室。

"我不该说谎，"他说，"我的小狗没有吃掉我的作业，是我自己没有做作业，不过现在已经做完了。对不起。"

"很好，谢谢你，亚瑟。"校长微笑着回应。

24. 整整一天，亚瑟都很开心，直到晚饭时候，他问爸爸："我们吃什么？"

"酸白菜！"爸爸回答。